◆ HOW TO ROCK CLIMB SERIES ◆

Sport Climbing

John Long

CHOCKSTONE PRESS

Evergreen, Colorado

COVER PHOTO:

Paul Piana on "Forbidden Colors," Mount Rushmore, South Dakota. Photo by Beth Wald.

BACK COVER PHOTO: Lynn Hill at Buoux, France. Photo by Beth Wald.

All uncredited photos by Kevin Powell.

ISBN 1-57540-078-2

PUBLISHED AND DISTRIBUTED BY
Chockstone Press, Inc.
Post Office Box 3505
Evergreen, Colorado 80439

OTHER BOOKS IN THIS SERIES:
How to Rock Climb!
Climbing Anchors
Advanced Climbing
Big Walls
Flash Training!
Knots for Climbers
Nutrition for Climbers
Building Your Own Indoor Climbing Wall
Clip and Go!
Self-Rescue
More Climbing Anchors
Top-Roping
How to Climb 5.12

Acknowledgements

SPORT CLIMBING

JOHN LONG

Credit to all those who wrote something for this manual: Rick Accomazzo, Dan Cauthorne, Scott Cosgrove, Hans Florine, Bob Gaines, Mari Gingery, Christian Griffith, Darrell Hensel, Lynn Hill, Eric Hörst, Troy Mayr, Alison Osius, Kevin Powell, Nancy Prichard, Duane Raleigh, Dr. Mark Robinson, John Sherman, and Russ Walling. Most agree that they learned something by putting into words what had long been instinctual. I trust we'll all be better climbers for their efforts. Likewise, thanks to photographer/climber Kevin Powell for his efforts over many weekends to provide those extra shots. Many thanks also to Mike Clelland for the fine line drawing on page 136.

Gia Phipps Franklin took the last edition and spent several months scouring every word. Gia's contributions were invaluable in helping to bring the language and techniques up to the cutting edge. Thank you.

WARNING: CLIMBING IS A SPORT WHERE YOU MAY BE SERIOUSLY INJURED OR DIE

READ THIS BEFORE YOU USE THIS BOOK.

This is an instruction book to rock climbing, a sport which is inherently dangerous. You should not depend solely on information gleaned from this book for your personal safety. Your climbing safety depends on your own judgment based on competent instruction, experience, and a realistic assessment of your climbing ability.

There is no substitute for personal instruction in rock climbing and climbing instruction is widely available. You should engage an instructor or guide to learn climbing safety techniques. If you misinterpret a concept expressed in this book, you may be killed or seriously injured as a result of the misunderstanding. Therefore, the information provided in this book should be used only to supplement competent personal instruction from a climbing instructor or guide. Even after you are proficient in climbing safely, occasional use of a climbing instructor is a safe way to raise your climbing standard and learn advanced techniques.

There are no warranties, either expressed or implied, that this instruction book contains accurate and reliable information. There are no warranties as to fitness for a particular purpose or that this book is merchantable. Your use of this book indicates your assumption of the risk of death or serious injury as a result of climbing's risks and is an acknowledgement of your own sole responsibility for your climbing safety.

C O N T E N T S

SPORT
CLIMBING

JOHN LONG

*Ian Spencer-Green on
"Deeper Shade of Soul,"
13b, Shelf Road,
Colorado.*

Stewart M. Green photo

It's Just
A Book

With the help of a handful of America's outstanding climbers, we serve up a little bag of helpful tricks that should improve your face/sport climbing. But for the best explanations, every climber is, essentially, self-taught. You learn how to face climb by face climbing. Period. As you climb more, you intuitively learn how to best perform. Though you may not be aware of every subtle move and technique, your body knows. So the value of this manual is that by studying the following material and by actually climbing, you can gain a new, or clearer, understanding of techniques which, to some extent, you already know and already are using in your climbing. The point is to become consciously aware of and understand all the basic principles, to verify what your body already knows, or eventually will learn. By stamping the precepts of good technique into your memory, your conscious awareness of them is increased as is your likelihood of using them. So, in this sense, this book can serve, at the least, as a sound reminder.

PERSPECTIVES

Climbing involves (amongst others) physical, strategic, mechanical and psychological aspects. An intimate, working relationship with each aspect is necessary to become a well rounded, successful climber. Neglect one aspect and you'll waste energy at best, and flounder at worst. The goal is to synchronize these aspects and bring holistic artillery to your game.

Correct climbing helps integrate both right (emotional) and left (logical) brain functions, and so opens up a path to experiencing wholeness. Climbing also involves the whole gamut of experiences. Climbing can take you to the stars, and dump you on your ass. However, when things get tough, if you keep perspective and realize that every move is a miracle, you'll be able to better appreciate all that climbing has to offer. Once you start pushing personal limits, climbing becomes an intense, committing activity. In one sense, climbing shows you who you are and what you're made of. No need to tackle the world's bleakest routes to know how it feels to be on top. Just climb, and you will know.

ASPECTS

The physical aspect starts with technique: footwork, body positioning, and various tricky tactics that help you to muster

Brett Spencer-Green on "Grapefruit Dance," 12a, Garden of Gods.

Stewart M. Green photo

through strange, difficult and oftentimes beautiful climbing. Then there's the strength factor, which includes three primary forms; pure (brute) power, strength endurance (how long you can maintain a maximum or near-max effort), and pure endurance (how long you can last, period). A recurring theme throughout this manual is that the best results come from using strength in concert with suave technique and body positioning.

Strategy helps you to assess the climb you're on or about to climb, and the moves you're doing or are setting up to do. Likewise, strategy helps you learn how to pace yourself both on and off the rock (preparing for what you want to do). All of these aspects will be taken up in great detail later on.

GENERAL SAFETY

Last but not least is the purely mechanical aspect—which concerns gear and ropework. Gear and ropework are your protection, providing a relative safety net when your pushing your limits or just grooving at the crags. Take this mechanical aspect for granted and get ready for the Pearly Gates. Make a major error with the mechanical and you ride on luck; and luck has passed by many of the most deserving, and experienced, individuals. There's an old saying: Luck carries no one on her shoulders for long.

Without a clear and thorough grasp of the mechanics of climbing, you're better off not play the game at all lest you get killed, or kill someone else. Again, this has happened to some of the best, most adept climbers, as well as some of the most inexperienced. Never think it won't happen to you; use extreme caution when climbing. Remember, the climbing game is for keeps. One reckless, forgetful move, and the curtain falls. Use caution every time you tie in, every time you belay, every time you place gear, every time you use your rope, every time you buckle in, and every time you rig anchors. Climbing is dangerous. Any time you go up, you have to come down, it's just a matter of how.

Often neglected as automatic, belaying must be performed with utmost seriousness. Remember, each time you belay you have someone else's life in your hands, as they have your life in their hands when belaying. Never forget that.

MINDFUL

The ability to stay on top of every step of every climb is called mindfulness, or presence of mind; strive to always have it and use it, and you'll go far. Without it, you're walking a highwire with no net.

Each aspect in climbing can be considered separately but

Wolfgang Schweiger at Eldorado Canyon, Colorado.

Beth Wald photo

without total integration, you are limited. So use this book as a guide, absorb everything in it that makes sense to you, and question everything that does not. Concoct your own solutions.

Inform and educate yourself. Get that triple Ph.D. in climbing, a process that is questionably the most wild education you'll likely get anywhere.

Protection fundamentals were laid down in *How to Rock Climb!,* and developed more thoroughly in *Anchors,* and *More Climbing Anchors.* Consequently, it is inappropriate to restate what has been done to death in other manuals of the How To Rock Climb! series. But keeping abreast of current gear and ropework tricks is an ongoing job. Read the magazines and equipment catalogs, and keep your eyes and ears peeled for the latest developments. Stay mindful and open to anything that might amplify your climbing experience.

Todd Skinner climbing at
Baldwin Creek,
Wyoming.

Beth Wald photo

Philosophy, History, The Future

The physical act of climbing, with its general movements and goals (getting to the top, be it of a 10-foot boulder, a 100-foot sport route or summiting on El Capitan) remains basically the same. However, the climbing community has grown ten-fold in the last decade. Such a deep tap of the global talent pool has shot standards over the moon. A dozen years ago, sport climbing was in its infancy. Breakthroughs were happening by the month. Presently, sport climbing has graduated from crawling; now we're learning how to walk.

At the outset, sport climbing had little if any direction other than a quest for higher difficulty. A scientific approach was, for the vast majority, totally lacking. Many people were first drawn to climbing owing to a perceived daredevil factor.

Twenty years ago, most top climbers were fringe dwellers, people with great athletic talents who didn't fancy traditional American sports, such as football, etc. Many were loners, misfits and renegades. As sport climbing emerged, competition climbing was born, which in turn opened a new door in climbing. Advanced training methods quickly evolved. The rebellious element is still alive in climbing, but the orientation has changed as the sport has continued to drawn from all walks of life and from many different countries.

INTERSTELLAR STANDARDS

Thirty years ago, 5.12 seemed an impossible standard. Anyone who could climb even occasionally at the 5.10 standard was considered heroic. Currently there are a handful of climbers who have "on-sighted" (climbed on his first try, with no previous knowledge) hard 5.13s, and Swiss stallion, Elie Chevieux, recently became the first to on-sight 5.14. As of this writing, 5.14d is the hardest grade yet achieved.

Several individuals have made great contributions to the the evolution of sport climbing. Examples include Lynn Hill's first all-free ascent of the Nose route on El Capitan, the most famous and sought-after rock climb in the world. The year after she first freed "The Nose," she did it "De Nase"—in one day. No easy task. Not quite a sport climb (to anyone), Lynn took "The Nose" and transformed it into the "Mother of all sport routes." The historical significance is that she successfully approached an incredibly difficult, (mentally and physically) long, and grueling traditional route as a sport climb.

This one ascent points the direction for all future sport climbers: to take the skills acquired on small climbs and apply them to older, longer and much more committing traditional climbs. The playing field is wide open.

Another historic ascent—accomplished in 1995—was German Alex Huber's free ascent of the classic "Salathe Wall," also on El Capitan. Astonishingly, Huber had never crack climbed before he free climbed the mighty "Salathe." While American's had made the first free ascent several years prior, Huber became the first man to single-handedly ascend the route, leading every pitch and not having to virtually camp on the wall and boulder out the moves. This ascent further established that the technical skills acquired on sport climbs could be applied directly to titanic adventure climbs, and that said climbs could be ascended relatively clean, that is, without days spent aiding up the hardest pitches.

Few sport climbers are sufficiently focused and mentally prepared to tackle mammoth projects like El Cap. Nevertheless a handful of adventurous souls are out there busting it up on the 1,000+ foot walls, putting up spectacular sport routes, bolted and all.

John Bachar on "Latest Rage," 12b, Smith Rock, Oregon.

Beth Wald photo

GOODBYE POPS

Teenage kids with less than two years experience are starting to surpass their elders as though they were standing still (mainly in the competition arena, and to a lesser degree at the crags). In 1996, fifteen-year-old Chris Sharma won a national title, established a 5.14 route, as well as red pointing a 5.14. Katie Brown, also fifteen, has also won national titles and the first two international events she entered (competing with the best women in the world!), has climbed 5.13, and flashed V10 boulder routes in Hueco Tanks. As always, young blood infuses new life to the sport. Given that the learning curve has no signs of leveling off, what the future holds is anyone's guess. But whatever happens, the contributions of sport climbing are certain to play a vital role.

CHAPTER 3

The Basics

Each area, each climb and each move dictates different styles while offering infinite ways of using your body. A key thing to understand is that the climbing dictates what techniques to use. Trying to impose your favorite technique on an inappropriate climbing problem is a mistake, and the earmark of underdeveloped technique and inexperience. Bring everything you learn from one place to the next, and apply it. It's all relevant and valuable.

Climbing involves much more that doing pull-ups. In one sense it's an advantage to enter this sport relatively weak. The weak beginner is forced to learn technique, body positioning, strategy, and so forth. It's amazing, for instance, how much weight you can relieve from your arms by moving your hips a little to the left, or right, thrusting them towards, or away from the rock, thinking a few moves ahead, assessing the angles of the wall and size of holds you're climbing on, all in preparation to picking the upcoming moves. The key point is to experiment. Try many things, and don't be afraid to feel desperate: it helps you find good stances. Watch other people closely, whatever level they climb at. You can learn from each and every movement, and the greater your repertoire of moves, the deeper and more useful is your bag of tricks. A blessing of watching beginners is that you see graphically how not to do things. In reflecting on your own climbing, you're apt to discover how you might, in some manner or degree, make the same mistakes, which allows you to make adjustments. In this way, everyone is your teacher.

As you climb, focus on each movement. Every move is climbed one move at a time. A desperate need to succeed sometimes throws your focus too far ahead. The move at your nose is neglected and you pitch off. At the same time you must have a strategy and be prepared for upcoming moves. Without this awareness, you'll have no sense of pace, without

Ian Spencer-Green on "The Prow," Cochiti Mesa, New Mexico.
Stewart M. Green photo

which you have no chance at a route near or at your limit. Climbing, and getting through impossible-feeling moves, is one of the closest things to feeling magic because you are doing what seems impossible. It's a high you won't easily forget.

Succeeding

Many say that at the higher levels, climbing is 1% talent and 99% hard work. Most everyone is inherently a climber, as the activity is natural for all healthy kids. As we get older, we're checked by self-imposed limitations. Belief is key. Once you acquire adequate strength and technique, the mind is the most important player. Countless climbers can rip off dozens of fingertip pull-ups, say, but such power does not translate directly to climbing difficult routes. Again, it's normally an advantage to enter climbing with limited strength. The weak climber must rely on technique, problem solving, and a strong mind. Strength will come in time, and mastering skills remains a climber's greatest asset. However, many climbers plateau when strength becomes their limiting factor. That's the time to shift your training toward bouldering, working with weights and so forth to acquire balance and not strain your muscles and tendons. This is a tricky business to try and explain, but the quickest way for the novice to improve is to climb routes within his or her strength range and to focus on technique. With experience, your strength will improve. Eventually your technique will get ahead of your strength, and only then should you concentrate specifically on strength. To concentrate on acquiring strength from the outset is to go about the business ass-backwards—like a baseball player focusing on hitting home runs before he acquires a fluid, efficient swing.

Weakling Wins

A common scenario is to come into climbing weak, learn about technique and eventually realize you must now work on strength. So you go to the gym and build muscle, then you hit the crags and feel top heavy from the newfound brawn, your feet feeling not so nimble as months pass. Given your increased might, you must relearn technique. It's a continuous circle: Learning new tricks, learning to apply them and then reshaping your old tricks to match your new level of prowess. Consider this a game of integration; the longer you stay at it, the higher your ceiling goes.

GENERAL PRINCIPLES

Economical movement—the single most important factor in cranking difficult face climbs—is impossible without a strong, focused and relaxed mind. If you're feeling charged up, don't expend all your energy in the first ten feet. Husband your strength, and strive after efficient movement, using the least amount of energy every step of the way. Climbing with straight, rather than bent, arms (especially when resting) conserves vast watts of energy.

Shake Out

For pumpy routes, or when you're dead pumped and have to carry on (usually because there's no resting), quickly shake

Boone Speed on "Malvado," 13a, El Diablo Wall, American Fork, Utah.
Stewart M. Green photo

out your arm before reaching to the next hold. The technique is simple: You're clasping a hold with your right arm, and you're blasted. Before reaching up for the next grip, momentarily drop your left arm down (to release blood flow) before reaching up. Done fluidly and consistently, this technique can save the day and keep you going when the ship is sinking fast. Again, while resting or setting up for a move, drop your arms (usually one at a time, though there are those rare occasions when you can drop both at the same time, getting a no-hands rest) to let the blood get back into your arms. A major factor for your arms getting pumped and sore is due to lack of blood, or over-pumping of blood into the arm. However that sick pumped feeling can be relieved by dropping your arms— while at rest, or even when you are climbing. Remember to coordinate this de-pumping with exhaling as you shake your arm out; this accelerates the de-pumping and freshens the blood supply, as well as clearing your head. While at rests, switch arms back and forth, alternating the de-pumping process. At first you may have to shake out quickly, because it feels impossible to hold on. Here, alternate quickly until you get fresh blood back in your arms. As your strength returns, you'll be able to shake out for longer periods, washing out the lactic acid (the burn) and resupplying the given gun with fresh blood. The same holds true for feet: Shake them out. Keep the blood fresh.

Focus

Focus on the CLIMBING, not on FALLING. Realize that a thought can determine how you approach and deal with everything. Choose and use your thoughts and emotions to your advantage. Think success. It works. Try it and trust it. A common pitfall is tunnel vision, where a climber will see only what is just under his nose. Open your eyes and mind to possibilities, and you'll likely find a solution—like a foot hold to the left or right. Always scan the rock for options. The wall will reveal inobvious secrets providing you stay open and receptive to sometimes improbable answers.

Pacing

Think; move; prepare for upcoming moves; conserve and be prepared for cranking; commit; go for it. In rough form, these are the keys to pacing yourself. Even quaking should not deter or sabotage you. Shaking with exertion is normal, and it's entirely possible to climb long stretches while trembling like an Olympic lifter attempting a record weight. Keep going, and try to breathe-out the willies. Breathing! Never get surprised by sewing machine leg, a wrong sequence, a misguided thought. Keep your wits up and go where you thought you never could. Such is the magic of climbing.

Mechanical Savvy

Verifying that your belayer/spotter is on the ball provides the the freedom to believe in the impossible, and to take the chances necessary to succeed. You may fall (safely), but most likely you'll learn from your mistakes. Belief is crucial when working near your limit. Watch everyone. You can learn from the total beginner to the most advanced climbers. Take in all the information you can. Watching others helps your body integrate new movements. There are endless different body positions and styles, so remain open and receptive to all the myriad options. Never pigeon-hole yourself. Soak everything up.

Scrunched

Avoid getting too stretched out, which compromises your center of gravity and consumes power to both hang on and extend out of a knot. Make small, relaxed moves whenever possible. An extremely high step can sometimes cop you a much-needed rest, but continuing on may be impractical and require more strength than that just saved. Same goes for stemming. Whenever possible, avoid splaying your legs out at max breadth. Try and keep your legs stemmed with enough flex in them that you can utilize your muscles.

At times you must squeeze hard to stay on. Here, leg power is key in sending energy throughout your body. Strive to integrate muscular tension/energy to all parts of the body, while at the same time relaxing your mind and breathing fluidly. Your abs are the crucial link in keeping your body in control and allowing energy to pass from the tips of your fingers down through your toes. (Try and feel this energy coming from the depths of your mind, and you'll soon realize that your mind is boss.) Oftentimes you'll see climbers with weedily legs and Herculean guns. Such a poor balance usually results in overgripping. Balance is key. Mind, body, emotions, motivation.

Souped Up

When souping up for the lead, if you feel hesitant, consider climbing up a ways and taking a short, calculated fall. This often helps to overcome the pre-leading jitters. Assess the situation smartly, however. Learning to lead inside climbing gyms, with the gear so close together, is totally different than leading outside, where pro is (often) farther apart, where you have to both place it and clean it as well as rig anchors. Gym climbers should never venture outside until they know exactly what they're doing, or are climbing with someone experienced who is willing to show and teach them. Experience and modesty will keep you alive. Sport climbing is relatively secure, but as mentioned, anytime you go up you have to come down. It's just a matter of how.

Bobbi Bensman maintaining composure.

Beth Wald photo

Composure

Composure does not mean staying in perfect control. So long as you're safe and well protected, go for it. Many times you must thrutch though sequences, balls to the walls. It's exciting and invigorating to do so. Always trying to climb ultra-smooth is a sure way to remain on easy ground. If you can't climb while sketching, you'll never crack the "impossible." Safety first, then go wild. Strive to climb smoothly, yes; but when you hit desperate straights, carry on no matter how shaky you feel (providing it's safe). Sketching past near "out of there" situations is the high water mark in every climber's career. Stay focused and prepared to pounce if you have to.

In ultra-pumpy situations, deep dig into your bag of tricks. Squeeze; shift your balance; work that body position; turn a straight down pull into an undercling or side pull. Get creative. Get dynamic if need be. A well-rounded climber is he or she who, through experience, has acquired more options to tackle hairball situations, and has the confidence to try them when the odds of success feel low. Your options will expand naturally if you exercise your right to fight.

Sequence

In many ways, climbing resembles a complex, sometimes syncopated dance. The rock is your teacher/choreographer and will continuously throw surprises your way. Be prepared for vastly funky moves, followed by smooth grooving sections. Stay malleable, and learn to flow from one mode of cranking to another. Whatever the climb dictates. And pace yourself. If a climb is flowing like the Blue Nile, then suddenly becomes thrutchy and awkward, stay composed and flow past the snags. As soon as the sequence mellows, return to smooth movement. Sounds obvious, but it's surprising how often climbers keep sketching long after they've passed over bleak street. It's sort of like a hangover, or a physical echo. Try and transition back to smooth grooving as soon as possible, which requires a mind open enough to recognize and respond to changes in the flow. The saying goes: Don't fight it, climb it. No use balking at climbs that aren't 100% flow, because very few are. Variety allows us to employ many different moves and thoughts to succeed.

Batting Practice

The value of experience cannot be overstated. If you have climbed quite a few 5.9 climbs, for example, another 5.9 route, while perhaps challenging, should not surprise you with its technical difficulties. You know you're up for the task, which bolsters confidence. And never underestimate the importance of climbing easier routes as well, the crag equivalent of a baseball player taking batting practice. Think of the Yankee centerfielder who takes hours of batting practice every week. The batting-practice pitcher just lobs the ball over the plate— it's like a 5.2 climb for a 5.11 climber— but the hitter can fully concentrate on the mechanics of his swing because the situation is much more controlled. If he faces only game-speed pitching, if he's always pressed to his maximum, he'll eventually lose form and slump. This is one of the problems facing the hotshot whose only interest is in scaling the hardest routes. If he sticks just to the bleak stuff—the "live pitching" if you will—his technique will improve slower than if he were to spend some time every outing doing easier climbs, settling into a comfortable flow and rhythm, and experiencing the mastery of climbing something flawlessly. It's like hammering meatballs over the fence and feeling like Barry Bonds in doing so.

Warm Up

If you get extremely pumped before warming up, your juices aren't flowing well enough to rinse out the burn (lactic acid), and the "flash pump" is the result. The effects will linger for hours; you might never shake a premature burn the entire

Bobbi Bensman climbing in Penitente Canyon, Colorado.

Beth Wald photo

day. So warm up well. Virtually every sport considers a warm up vital not only to perform efficiently, but to avoid injuries. And since few if any sports put such stress on the sinews and joints as climbing does, an adequate warm up is crucial. Each climber arrives at her own process, but several things remain constant:

Always start on something easy to moderate. This allows you to get your head together, warms up your finger joints and tendons, gets your movement flowing smoothly, warms up your dynamic movements and dead pointing skills, and focuses your eye-to-body coordination. It's essential for longevity to take care of your joints, impossible without a consistent and proper warm up.

Most climbers bag at least one warm up route, proceeded and followed by some stretching. Stretch your whole body; legs, arms, back, fingers, shoulders. Avoid overstretching via forced or painful yanking moves. Breathe deeply, and let the muscles slowly elongate under constant, but not punishing, tension. "Shock" stretching pumps you up needlessly, and often strains muscles. Take caution, but do stretch.

Once you've worked up a sweat and have gotten the blood flowing evenly throughout your limbs, you're ready to fire. For those recovering with injuries, particularly elbow tendonitis and tendon/joint inflammation or tweaks, don't start cranking until stiffness and pain have been worked through. The "grin and bear it" school of climbing has ended, or put on hold, many climbing careers, including mine (J.L.).

Flexibility

Tiffany Levine defines hip turn-out on the wall at Snowbird, Utah.

Beth Wald photo

To climb well you need to be loose. The handhold you're cranking off often becomes your next foothold. Walls with textured or sculpted relief occasionally offer wee intermediate holds, but often there's nothing, save for a bleak friction press between holds. This means high-stepping is a crucial practice. And high-stepping requires flexibility. Regular stretching, like the basic exercises you've been doing since junior-high gym class, are fine for getting started, but to really step high requires specific exercises.

To work your hip turn-out flexibility, try scrunch traverses. Set a string of handholds and footholds close together and just off the ground. The notion is to keep your knees scrunched up around your hands, and your hips close in to the wall. Avoid using jugs for your hands. Good handholds will let you lean your upper body out, and in doing so cheat the stretch. A well-set scrunch traverse uses sloping handholds which force you to keep your chest and hips in close to the wall.

Also, set up and practice specific high-step situations. On a vertical wall, place two sloping handholds (again, slopers keep you honest) about head high. For the footholds, mount a ladder of good edges leading up to the handholds. Get on the wall and practice walking your feet up the edges. When you think your feet can't go any higher, pause on the high footholds and relax for a couple of seconds. Relaxing will loosen up your groin and hips and buy you a couple more inches.

Another good high-step exercise involves placing jugs about chest level and then pulling up on them and replacing your hands with your feet. If this move is already easy for you, replace the jugs with slopers.

Rest Days

Rest days ensure longevity. Your fingers and upper body sustain great stresses, and need rest to recover and reknit. Your joints need rest. Your mind needs rest. Even your motivation needs rest. Without adequate rest, your learning curve will flatten out if not drop off the chart. For super active climbers, rest days don't necessarily mean total rest. A day of climbing cruiser routes (say, two to three grades below your limit) can build conditioning without blasting your cranking apparati. Same goes for cross-training. Nevertheless, some days must be spent doing nothing physical at all. Listen to your body. Avoid spending consecutive days working a route and maxing yourself. Alternate between endurance, strength, and strength endurance training. Mix it up and when you feel shot, call it off.

Limitations

Self-imposed limitations deter our progress. Avoid pigeon-holing yourself into a category. As we evolve, we broaden our repertoire of moves. If you're heavy, that doesn't mean you can't shred like the others. You're likely stronger than most climbers. At high level competitions you sometimes see large climbers send burly desperate routes. Same goes for age. Since climbing is not a reaction sport like tennis, or boxing or baseball, the older you get, the wiser, more mature and clear-headed you get. I've often heard climbers in their 40s and 50s say they have never been stronger. The point is, never let limits of labels interfere with your dreams. Overcome self-perceived limits; let yourself be free to explore, take chances, do the improbable. Try and get to that place where only the moves can defeat you, never your own mind.

Pitfalls

Even the greatest heroes have limitations. The frightening part is that while people are pulling down harder than ever, the occurrence of basic ropework blunders is alarmingly high.

The ability to crank hard does not translate to good judgement or safety. The camaraderie and friendly competition found in most gyms sometimes leads people to climb way past their mechanical level of competency. Kids can pull off 5.13s these days but most would be hard pressed to place a bomber anchor or lead a 5.10a adventure route. Get it: On adventure climbs (or any climb requiring self-placed pro), climbing past your mechanical level is dangerous, even deadly. So modesty, humility, and honesty should remain your guide on the rock. Boldness should never overshadow experience. Learn how to recognize and factor in potential risks, inside or out.

In the unforgiving world of rock (not gym) climbing, knowledgeable 5.7 climbers are normally far safer than 5.13 gym aces who lack time on real rock. Even if you're a diehard sport climber, learn all you can about gear and traditional climbing.

The number of avoidable accidents—some fatal—is higher than ever, and the reason is that people are trying to skip the crucial fundamentals of rope management and judgement that past generations picked up while working up through the grades on traditional adventure routes. While gym climbing has, for some, become an end in itself, it is for many only a training tool for tackling anything but dinky routes, no matter how high they are rated. Study your roots. Respect your sport. And when you want to transition into longer, traditional routes, do so only after you have the experience to do so safely, and when you know that you do.

TO BETA OR NOT TO BETA

"Betas" are blow-by-blow breakdowns of a given route. Casual betas are simply what one climber tells another, the narrative usually accompanied by lavish body contortions that physically describe the climbing. Formal betas can be fabulous for their detail, and sometimes are drafted on graph paper with an attending written drift of the rarest crag lingo. The generic information is almost always useful, but beyond that, be careful when trying to execute the beta to the letter. You're glad to know that you should layback here, or reach for the hidden bucket there, but don't force yourself into a sequence that doesn't feel right.

Many times at the crag you'll hear folks screaming at each other for beta. Sometimes the beta is unsolicited—just someone trying to be helpful and wailing directions at a stranger or friend. Again, the vast differences in body types, strengths and brains, makes it impossible to give exact beta, even for people the same size. Some climbers despise beta because it robs them of figuring things out for themselves and interrupts their flow. These climbers usually excel at firing sequences and relish the opportunity to do so. Others love beta because it helps them get through cruxes with less hassle, or without having to think too much. Many consider beta essential only when they are climbing at their physical limit and cannot spare a second or a watt of juice to think and reckon a sequence. For these reasons, beta is usually reserved for super strenuous routes, for relative beginners, or for those trying to dash up through the grades. Beta is best used when you are completely stymied on a route and can't make progress. If you're stuck at a crux, you can pull past, figure out the rest of the route while you still have energy and skin, then go back to the parts that spanked you and suss them out. Then rest and send your project.

STRATEGY

On most any face climb, you can conceive a workable strategy by eyeballing the pitch. That's because vertical and overhanging climbs have features (lest you'd never be able to climb them), so you can see what you are up against. Not so on slab and edging routes, where the climb is often bald, and leaders have a hard time seeing holds that are right in front of their faces. Be prepared for anything and everything. There are considerations other than cranking the actual moves that should be factored into the equation—like gear placements and potential falls. Assess all factors. With experience you'll be able to tell much from a quick glance.

Shrewd Counsel

In preparing for a climb that you are not intending to on-sight, find out what the climb entails, what the moves and protection are like, where the crux is, etc. What you hear from one source is bound to differ from a second source. Best to get a stack of opinions. From them all, you usually can draw a useful, general picture of the climb. Guidebook topos are useful for generic information and tend to be more objective. But many times it's these subjective, first-hand accounts that give you the best "vibe" about what to expect.

MODES OF ASCENT

With many modern routes, the goal is to get to the top of the route, not necessarily the cliff. Many times you will climb to the anchors; sometimes you may not. Sometimes it may take you several attempts to figure out a particular move/crux. A crux signifies the most difficult section or move on a climb. There may also be

Ed Strang belays Brett Spencer-Green on "Child of Light," 13d.

Stewart M. Green photo

several stopper moves. One of the brilliant aspects about climbing is that what once seemed impossible, with some work and figuring, may well prove possible once you start to work. Free climbing is about climbing a route without using any artificial points of gear—no pulling on the rope, no tension, just you, your belayer, gear, the route and your body. An ascent is not considered "free" until the climber can scale the route, bottom to top, without falling. Sounds like a black-and-white affair, doesn't it? In practice, however, the means by which a climber eventually leads the pitch may involve the most dazzling chicanery. That acknowledged, a loose set of terms has evolved that explains exactly what means were used. And the means can make all the difference.

Note that while the end has often come to justify the means of ascent, the closer a climber comes to performing the on-sight flash, the more celebrated his effort is considered. So it's safe to say that the mode of ascent will remain important to climbers, as it should.

Following are some of the terms we use in free climbing.

On-sighting: No beta (information) at all, except for the grade. The minute you start milking any information, you've blown your on-sight and are looking to do a good flash ascent.

Flashing: Consists of obtaining knowledge of the route about to be ascended for the very first time. You could learn one crucial piece of information, or be talked all the way up the route; you could have only watched someone on it. If you have seen or heard anybody talking about or climbing the route you are attempting, you are not on-sighting, rather trying a flash ascent (providing it's your first time on it). Flashing is not as difficult as on-sighting a route of the same level.

Deja vue: You've been on the route a long time ago, don't remember much about it and are going for it. It may feel like you've never been on it, but you have. Basically what it sounds like.

Red point: Could be a seized route you've been trying for years, or a close flash, or an on-sight that had to get red pointed on your second try. Basically climbing a route without falls after you've been on it once or many times.

Yo yo: You try to red point, you leave gear fixed on the route—like for instance a top rope is set up above the crux and then you lead the last two bolts.

Top rope: Climb without potential of falling on lead. Generally risk free climbing. A free ride.

There are many ways to ascend a climb. The purest, albeit most dangerous, way being on-sight soloing: climbing a route without any rope or gear and with no prior knowledge of the route. This is a perilous practice, which only your worst enemy would recommend. More on free soloing later.

Climbing with a rope, a good belayer, good gear, and a strong working knowledge of climbing, is the smartest way to get to the top and come back for more. Think long term. Think safety.

Responsibilities

When you're swinging leads, you have someone else's life in your hands 50% of the time; the other 50% you're in someone else's hands. It's our responsibility to accept this, and to admit our shortcomings, despite our great strengths. And to learn as much as possible. We have to take care of this great thing we do. It can take us to many realms and dimensions. It enlivens our minds for problem solving, our bodies for strength, technique, balance, our emotions for motivation, our spirits for thankfulness and appreciation. With such an extreme, total sport/activity, it bodes strongly to take care of each and every step we take.

Razors Rip My Flesh

You only have so many razor cranks in you at a given time.

Bird Lew on "Embrace This," 5.11d, Owens River Gorge, California.

Kevin Powell photo

That is, your fingertips wear out before your muscles do. You'll want to build up those callouses, either on the boulders or by doing hard edging routes—preferably by doing both. One famous climber draws a bastard-file over his fingertips during off-days, though I don't advise this technique. No matter how tough your fingertips are, a hard, sustained edging route can shred them. The most common gash is a "split tip," where the skin parts in frown-like fashion along the thin arc-

Didier Raboutou on "Les Byiuts des Lisards," 8a, Buoux, France.

Beth Wald photo

ing line of a fingerprint. These are painful, and take up to two weeks to fully heal. Attempts to "Crazy-Glue" split tips back together have been somewhat successful, but this is a stop-gap measure that only leads to more serious injury. Once you cut through to the dermis, the genuine meat, you'd best lay off for a while. Or go with cracks for a spell. And, contrary to what you might think, keep those cracked and split fingers well oiled. A dab of Vaseline, Neosporin, or Bag Balm (the antiseptic vets use on cow udders) will heal them quicker. Dry skin only keeps cracking.

Climbing a route taking as few falls as possible precludes you from having to repeat hard, painful moves and cutting your fingers to ribbons—another reason to work up a good strategy before tackling the lead.

A note on joint care: Chinese Iron Medicine Balls are particularly effective in keeping joints strong and limber. Stretching your fingers—together and individually—is very important to opening up your hand.

A NOTE ON SHOES AND FOOTWORK

Most major shoe companies make excellent shoes for precise footwork. The key is to find the shoes that best fit your foot. Try on tons of pairs to find the right one. Most serious climbers have a quiver of different shoes for different types of climbs. Stiff shoes are good for technical edging. Slippers are good for developing toe and foot strength, as well as building confidence in your footwork. Good footwork is at the root of good climbing. Take advantage of every chance to develop strong feet and deft footwork, and you'll feel like a magician. As your feet get stronger, you may find that softer, more sensitive shoes will allow you to really work the stone. In time your foot learns to manipulate the rock through a sensitive shoe. It's amazing how well you'll be able to edge on technical routes with a soft shoe/slipper.

Having different shoes for different climbs helps to preserve your shoes, and for you to get more out of each climb and shoe. You don't need painfully tight shoes to get ultimate precision, but you do want to fit the shoe as snugly as you can reasonably handle. For steep routes, go with a shoe that you can heel hook and toe hook in, something with a solid, sturdy heel. A lace up model works well. More on that in the steep climbing section.

Pure Sole

Keep your boots clean—the soles, anyway. The vast majority of modern "sticky rubber" rock soles are not rubber at all, but a petroleum-based synthetic (TDR, or thermo-dynamic rubber), which is a magnet for grease, pine sap, etc. Don't hike about in your $150 boots. Carry a toothbrush-sized wire brush in your pack, and spend thirty seconds before a climb giving your soles the once over. No need to submit your boots to Clorox ablutions, resins, emery boards, et al. A couple passes with the wire brush (water or spit also works) and your boots will perform like they're supposed to.

CHAPTER 4

Technique

All good technique hinges on balance: physical balance; balance of your strength and climbing style; balance between motivation and shrewd pacing. Balance is your friend, your teacher, your guide. Pay attention to what balance requires of you, asks from you, and gives to you. You will gain much.

FOOTWORK

There are infinite ways to use your feet while climbing, but whatever the position and method, foot placement is about precision, subtly, decisiveness, balance, and commitment. Footwork is the foundation that your climbing is based on, and propitious boot placement—the ability to place the boot precisely on the hold—comes only with experience.

THINK small

When you've a choice, make two smaller moves rather than one long one. This is particularly important to those just getting acquainted with hard face climbing. Keep making unnecessary high steps and the dreaded "sewing-machine leg" will soon kick in, where your legs start quaking like you're climbing toward the electric chair. Stick with the smaller moves whenever possible. Less work, better balance—better climbing all around.

EDGING

Climbers generally prefer to edge with the big toe, right where the nail cuts back. This "great toe" posture is pretty much the standard edging position on perhaps 70% to 80% of all edging moves. The footholds will dictate what part of your foot to use and how much pressure you should apply. The able edger can edge with any part of his boot—even the heel—because there are many situations where the foothold is not clear-cut or dead horizontal. The position of the edge, relative to your body position, determines what part of the boot you will edge with. The general idea is to edge wherever it feels most natural. You can go only so far using the "great toe" edge, so get accustomed to using whatever part of the boot the move or climb requires.

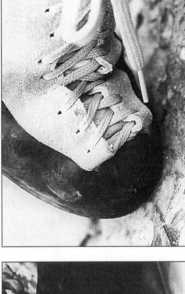

(opposite)
Bill Hunt on "Alta World".
Craig Dillon photo

Didier Raboutou crank-
ing on his outside edge,
Snowbird, Utah.

Beth Wald photo

Outside Edging

Learning to edge with the outside of your foot is a crucial
technique for diagonal reaching, for gaining extra reach, for
relieving stress on your forearms, and when utilizing holds
that would otherwise require unnatural body positioning. Get
sideways, with your hip pressed next to the wall and the outside edge of your foot pressed precisely onto the hold. The
main concern is to stay in balance. Outside edging can work
well when your leg is bent; this helps to relieve even more
stress on the arms. Another effective technique is to bring
your leg/foot across the inside of your body, so that it's in a
diagonal attitude relative to your reaching arm. That is, if
you're reaching with your right arm, your right hip is pressed
into the rock, while your right leg is crossed in front of your
body, next to the wall. Smearing with the outside of your edge
is also effective. Balance and preserving strength is key.

Outside edging/smearing is also effective to rest tired feet
on holds that otherwise would pump your calves even worse.

While edging—as with any foot work—maintain pressure,
weight, and energy throughout the foot and body. Once the
foot is placed, pasted or smeared, keep it there, applying constant pressure until you're ready to move on. Remember, the
pressure you apply, especially if it's a dicey placement, may
need to be minutely readjusted. Do not keep tapping the foot
on the hold.

Place it definitively to begin with. If you feel your boot but-
tering off, precisely, subtly, and directly reapply pressure.

When you go onto the next move, use your eyes and precisely place your foot on the hold or position you select. Commit. Be confident. Believe in the improbable; that's part of what precision edging is all about.

Steep Edging

Steep edging entails strength, precise footwork and the ability to quickly figure out and execute obscure moves. Throughout you must stay balanced on often tenuous holds, enduring extreme muscular tension and maintaining controlled relaxation/breathing.

On ill-defined holds, you may not get the purchase required to master the move, so keep in mind the myriad of ways to use your feet creatively, and wield your weapon with intelligence and intuition.

Front Pointing

Using the front point of the boot is useful and necessary for pockets, and sometimes for very small edges. It also comes into play on big edges. If your feet are unusually strong, the heel can be kept low; but most climbers hinge the heel up slightly when point edging. Unless the edge is down-sloping, the heel most always is higher than the toe.

Pocket footwork is the same as any, but poses the added problem that since pockets don't protrude, they are hard to see once they get down around knee level. For that reason, make a concerted effort to memorize the location of each pocket as you climb by it.

A good trick to save time and energy is to put a dab of chalk above seemingly critical footholds as your face passes them. Move up and simply toe in just below the dot and you're in business.

On vertical walls, you'll want to toe directly into the hole and press off, much the same way that ice climbers employ "front pointing." The pocket size will dictate how much boot will go in, but boots with pointed, flat toes naturally get a better bite than boots with round or bulbous toe boxes. When you're on overhanging rock, make a conscious effort to press your toes into the bottom of the pocket, or curl them against the inside walls and pull with them just as you would your fingers. A soft, slipper-type shoe works best here, but forget about using your five-year-old Ninjas which are way stretched out and have been resoled ten times—just too sloppy to work well. Instead, go with a pair of slippers with sling-shot heel rands.The tight, sensitive glove-like fit will allow your big toe to work some miracles for you on those overhanging pocketed walls. Remember, only through immaculate use of your feet will you be able to create the body tension and torque necessary for keeping your body close to the rock. Body position is everything on steep rock, and it's your feet that "work" the positions. So get a pair of shoes that don't penalize you from the start.

Tim Fairfield on "White Queen," 13b, Babies Wall, Enchanted Tower, New Mexico.

Stewart M. Green photo

Cobble It

If you think cobbles make slick handholds, wait until you step on them. Some climbers don't like the balancey, insecure feel of cobbles, and make a point to avoid them. No need if you understand the following maxims for basic cobble footwork. First, wear a soft shoe with good rubber. Stiff shoes don't mold to the knob, and old rubber is drier and slicker than newer stuff. Second, stay in the shade (a good rule for most types of climbing)—cobbles get alarmingly greasy in the sunlight, adding a notch or two to the route's difficulty. Finally, set your feet carefully, load the hold slowly to test your purchase. And keep those feet rock steady. Start quivering and you're a sure goner. Greased, polished cobbles are scary articles for everyone.

STEMMING

Stemming, or "bridging," is the process of counter-pressuring with the feet off slanting holds. The classic stem problem occurs in right-angled corners, where the climber must ratchet his limbs up via counter-pressure. Often, the applied pressure is improbable and marginal, particularly on steep face routes, where the holds are often sloping. And it's not just a task for the feet. The hands must counter-pressure against the holds. Essentially, your body is like a spring, loaded between two opposing holds. The only thing holding the spring in place is the purchase at both ends and the tension between them. Moving the spring up, then, is the tricky bit, as the tension must go lax for a second. Yet it never can. Often it is the diagonal pressure of one hand against one foot that keeps you on the wall, and the climber alternates this bridge in moving up. The variations are endless: you may back-step with one boot and smear with the other, or palm with one hand and crimp a dime with the other. Flexibility and balance

Mark Hudon is an "Aggro Monkey," Smith Rock, Oregon.

Laird Davis photo

are key. And supple ankles a must. Many times the stem is less valuable in gaining height than it is in gaining a quasi-rest. If you can manage a solid stem on a steep route, it gives you a good foundation to shake each arm out in turn, snatch a breath, and survey what's ahead. The art of stemming is a tricky one, and the practice becomes less and less likely as the angle steepens.

KNEE LOCKS AND BARS, HEEL AND TOE HOOKS

Locks, bars and hooks have become very common practices for climbing the steep terrain. These techniques have always been around but have earned greater recognition and are required for today's routes, particularly in roof climbing. Steep and horizontal roof climbing looks impossible and intimidating, but with proper body positioning and knee locks, toe hooks, and heel hooks it's truly amazing how far one can go. The difference between employing or not employing these specialized tricks is as extreme as not even being able to make a single move, to actually climbing long routes with your legs, abdominals and arms like crazy.

Feet

Your feet perform two essential functions on overhanging rock: supporting your lower torso, and providing push for upward movement. Realize that if your feet are not placed properly or hooked on something, you'll be left hanging entirely from your arms—the worst position on an overhanging route. With feet dangling, the mightiest arms burn out in a matter of yards. Generally look for and utilize a combination of both hooks and pushing footholds. First, the hooks. There will be places for your feet, though you'll have to work at finding the most secure spots. Let's start with the really overhanging stuff—routes steeper than 120 degrees.

Because much of your body is back and under your hands, gravity wants to peel your feet off any hold and leave you hanging straight up and down, directly under your gassed arms. Consequently, there always is a constant pull on your feet, as though boulders were attached to your heels. Carefully placing your foot on a good edge guarantees nothing. On routes just over vertical, this is not so much a problem. But once the angle starts to kick back, you must get your foot lodged or hooked for the foot to help your upward progress.

Doing The Frog

As mentioned, on vertical-to-overhanging face climbs, it's physically impossible to keep your center of gravity directly

Todd Skinner "Throwing the Hoolihan," 14a.

Beth Wald photo

over your feet. The aim is to use your feet in ways that will relieve the stress on your arms, and assist in thrusting you up. This requires keeping your hips sucked into the wall. There are two main ways to accomplish this: with "frog-style" turnout, and by back stepping, or knee dropping.

For the frog move, splay your hips wide, and keep them as close to the wall as flexibility allows. Ideally, while pressing your weight up, your hips will follow a straight line close to the wall. If you have poor turn-out flexibility, your hips will be further from the wall, forcing more weight onto your hands and arms. A stretching regimen will greatly enhance your turn-out flexibility.

Back Step

When making long reaches on overhanging turf, back stepping is particularly effective. This technique also works well when the handholds are side pulls or underclings. To back step, turn sideways to the rock and stand on the outside edge of one foot and the inside edge of the other. The hip above the back-stepped foot is twisted into the rock to get weight on your feet. When moving your left hand up, say, you'll normally (though not always) back step with your left foot. This provides stability between the left foot and the locked-off right hand. After grabbing the left handhold, you'll sometimes rotate your backstep the other direction, so you can reach up with the right hand.

Cheops

When the footholds face each other, a variation on the back step is the knee drop—also called the "Egyptian." The knee drop pulls the center of gravity closer to the feet, thereby easing the load on your hands. It also creates opposition between the feet, similar to stemming. Knee dropping is to the '90s what manteling was to the '70s. Sitting in a deep knee drop can provide a superb forearm rest, even on the steepest rock.

Figure-4

Because falls out of figure-4s are explosive and often head first, make sure you have either a good spotter or a top-rope before trying to learn this technique. That done, proceed. Grab a jug with your right hand (or left hand if that's what the move calls for). Pivot your torso around and wrap your left leg (right leg if you're holding on with your left hand) over your right arm so that the crook of your knee rests on your right wrist. To help stabilize yourself, try to edge with your feet. Now reach with your free hand. Easy huh?

Figure-4

When is a figure-4 called for? This move is extremely taxing and hard on your wrist, so you won't find it often; when you do find one, it is usually the only way past that section, so it pays to learn it. The usual scenario is a jug, followed by a long blank section ending in a smallish hold that you couldn't latch with a regular lunge or dead point—this begs of figure-4. Roofs or radically steep walls are also likely terrains. Slabs, vertical walls, and slightly overhanging walls are out—they don't give your body enough clearance under the hold to let your hips swivel up and around. The figure-4 is usually performed as a kind of novelty or circus stunt. The times in which it is required are precious few, and it remains a last resort owing to the stress it puts on your fingers and wrist.

PERFECT MATCHING

"Matching" is the sharing of holds, the switching of one foot/hand on a hold to the other foot/hand. Matching takes various forms, and is a required technique on climbs of all ilks. Wiggle and maneuver your foot or hands/fingers carefully and subtly to replace with another body part. This works well when you get out of sequence, when the holds are sparse and you want to maximize your options, and when traversing. When matching on small holds you sometimes must sacrifice a perfect grip for something less, clasping a four finger hold with only three or two fingers, say, so the hand coming in to match has somewhere to grab. Jockeying the fingers around until the new hand is secure is often tense business as you caterpillar your digits while clinging for all your worth. Practice can impart the particulars of this important technique. The variations are as many as the stars in the sky.

GRIPS: UPPER BODY PULLING

Crimp it!

Crimping and open handed grips are the two standard methods used while face climbing. For pocket climbs, aretes, dihedrals, cracks and steep terrain, an infinite variety of grips derive from these two main themes. Creativity is crucial in maximizing your use of grips.

For strong fingers and hands—which get you up the routes—you need powerful contact strength. "Contact" strength is the amount of torque you can apply to a given hold, and can vary dramatically according to how your fingers are placed on an edge. So, the first and foremost concern is to grab the hold in the best spot, where you can apply the most crank. Experience is the key here, yet it's amazing how many seasoned climbers show little skill in precise hand placement. They simply grab the hold willy-nilly, then pull. Wrong. Any given hold, however uniform, affords a "best" position for your hands.

Your index and second (middle) finger are stronger than your ring finger and pinky. Try to get the former two digits well set on the best and sharpest part of the edge. It's a simple and almost instantaneous procedure: eyeball the edge, place your hand on it and before cranking, apply a little pull to the hold, quickly verifying your grip or juking your fingers around slightly to improve the purchase. Sometimes your thumb will snag a bump or edge, adding to the overall security of the hold.

Your strongest digit is your thumb—by far. This is why crimping is such a strong grip. By wrapping your thumb over the nail of your index finger, you enjoy at least a 20% boost in cranking might. For most people, the thumb will automatically wrap over the index finger; pulling on small holds will otherwise feel strange and imbalanced. However, if your thumb isn't long enough, or this technique feels awkward for you, relax. Some of America's most talented boulderers swear by the open grip, and, in fact, they probably experience fewer finger injuries.

Lastly, whatever grip you use, try to get the heel of the palm well-seated on the rock. This can get you additional purchase, via friction between palm and rock, but is not always possible. If it feels unnatural to bend your wrist in to get your palm on the rock, forget it. If it does feel okay, though, it's a boon.

Crimping has always been an important and popular grip for clasping small holds. Whether you're climbing a slab route, sheer face, arete, dihedral, steep route or even roof, you'll be able to crimp if there's a square enough edge to the hold (the hold can be tiny to large). The drawback with all crimping is that it taxes your joints. Iron Chinese balls that massage your hands by hitting acupressure points are invaluable tools in decreasing arthritis—a threat to every climber who crimps often and earnestly.

Open Hand

A sure way to reduce hand injuries and build strength is to use, whenever possible, an open handed grip. The open hand grip will feel weird and insecure to a novice, since you never lock onto the hold as you do when crimping. The advantages are that the open grip covers more surface area, allows you to use your thumb and fingers in tricky ways, and greatly reduces the occurrence of injuries occasioned by crimping. Though tenuous at first, the more you practice the open grip, the stronger you're hands will become. In time, the open grip will feel as bomber as crimping, even moreso on rounded holds.

The open grip came into its own only when sport climbing became the fad. Before, everyone crimped. Because many sport climbs follow rounded holds that cannot be crimped, the open hand grip was refined through necessity. Only later, after folks had mastered this grip, did they apply it success- fully to holds that were formerly crimped, and only after doing so was it discovered that most any hold (save for dime edges) can be open handed, and that doing so was a far gen-

Ian Spencer-Green on "Miror du Fou," Verdon, France.

Stewart M. Green photo

tler method on the joints and tendons. To mas- ter the open hand grip, you must practice it long and hard until the forearm muscles develop. This is a long-term project. Gains are slow, but they come in time.

Pockets

Pockets come in all sizes and dimensions, from extremely shallow and practically useless dim- ples, to slammer jammer finger engulfers. The fact that your fingers are very isolated while pocket climbing means you are prone to injury. Caution is the word when using pockets, espe- cially with "mono" (one-finger) pockets. While stuffing or fidgeting your fingers into a bomber pocket, take care to utilize your entire hand, your body positioning and foot work. All these help prevent joint damage, a very real threat on grievous pocket pulling.

Pockets often allow you to twist and stack your fingers to create a jamming effect, a truly

Wolfgang Schweiger pulling pockets at Shelf Road, Colorado.

Beth Wald photo

effective technique for pulling hard. They can also hurt you quickly owing to massive torque on those digits. Again, be careful. Experiment with different ways to work a pocket. By leaving a finger or two out of a pocket, placing them on surrounding rock and counter-pressuring them against the in-pocket pulling action, you can oftentimes gain extra leverage. You can also use your fingers on the outside of the pocket as a crimping help, along with the finger(s) inside the pocket.

Before tackling a savage pocket route, make certain you've warmed up and stretched your fingers. Also, for extreme pocket pulls that only take one or two fingers, you can reduce your chances of getting "twanged" by reinforcing the commonly injured tendon pulleys with three firm turns of tape around the base of each finger. As with any small (strenuous) hold you encounter, get on and off of those mono-doigts fast. You only have a few seconds to do a one-finger pull, so if you hang around thinking about it, you'll be off, or injured.

The type of grip you use when pulling pockets should be dictated by the pocket. Most common is the open-hand grip since it works best on neutral or sloping surfaces. However, when the pocket is incut or has a sharp edge, the crimp grip is often more comfortable and may allow you to latch onto the hold in such a way that you can pull it down to your side further than what is possible with an open grip. If the hold doesn't dictate a specific grip, then use the open hand, which is stronger and less stressful.

On the ubiquitous two-finger pockets, old crimp masters often place and yard with their index and middle fingers. However, people raised on pocket yanking normally go with the middle and ring finger, which provides a more balanced pull. Like open hand grips, this later technique requires practice, but that practice pays off with a smoother, more powerful grip in the end.

Finally, don't forget to use all 360° of the pocket. Unlike edge climbing, where you are generally pulling down on the holds, many pockets afford the option of using them as side pulls, underclings, and killer thumb mantles. When paired with a hip turn, back step, or drop knee, these hand positions can make a seemingly rad move quite mild. Forget these tricks and you might as well forget about climbing hard pocket routes.

Cobbles and Knobs

There are three basic ways to grab cobbles: dead-on, in a pseudo-crimp grip; the "pinky wrap," where you take the beef of your palm and pinky finger and wrap the hold; and the open hand. The optimum grip depends on the cobble's (or knob's) size, and how far it protrudes. Grab grapefruit-sized cobbles with the open-hand grip, just as you would a softball. When a cobble sticks out an inch or so, the pinky wrap is usually the ticket. This grip, while it feels insecure and takes time to master, is actually very powerful, yet doesn't require a lot of strength; in fact, in many cases you can "rest" from this grip. Treat smaller cobbles like edges: crimp them. When none of the above grips seem to work, try pinching the cobble between your thumb and forefinger. But go easy: the pinch grip rapidly drains your strength, and your fingers can abruptly spit off from this position.

Rosy Palms

On slabs and lower-angled edging routes, the features need not be large or well-defined to help our cause. This is particularly so with various palming maneuvers, where the hand is placed flat over, or against, an irregularity—a bump, wee shelf, or any roughly-textured spot often will do. When the angle is quite low, you actually can mantel off a well-placed palm, usually positioned with the fingers pointing straight down. More common is a lateral palm, where you press or lean off the palm for balance. Sometimes opposing palms can afford enough purchase, if only briefly, to move the feet up.

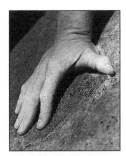

Rane Morris-Dunn on
"Patrick Hedgclipper,"
Castlewood Canyon,
Colorado.

Stewart M. Green photo

The most useful, and most common palm, is the one placed in a mantel position, while the other hand pulls on an edge. In most instances, both the edge and the palm are very marginal, and the move requires consummate balance, plus the ability to weight both holds just short of the point that they will skid off. On honestly grim cruxes, it's a case of all four limbs being poised on borderline holds. Oftentimes, the palm is the best of the four. In the absence of any edges to palm off, simply pressing the fingers of the palmed hand into tip-sized depressions is enough to stop the hand from skidding off.

Chalking for any of these palming moves is an art. Remember that it's the friction of the fingers and heel of the palm that provides the grab, and that too much chalk can reduce that friction. Use just enough to keep the palm dry, but not so much that you have a slippery layer between the palm and the doubtlessly poor hold.

Slabs, Vertical, Arêtes, Dihedrals, Steep, Overhanging, Roofs

CHAPTER 5

SLABS

Some of the most prestigious, bold, painful and entertaining routes (easy or hard) are found on slabs. Competency on slab routes improves you body positioning, balance, your method of clasping holds, hones your mental skills and produces "to-die-for" calf muscles. These skills translate to increased performance on all forms of cragging—from the slabs themselves, to overhanging gym routes.

No one can shine on the slabs without relaxing. For instance, needless tension will cause overgripping, the bane of fluid technique. On the slabs we learn subtley of body positioning is one of the keys for utmost performance and control. Bald slabs force you to focus, relax and move smoothly. Likewise, the often lengthy runouts between pro build strong minds.

The experienced slab hand moves like an ant—light and cool. At times you must lean and push and palm, use your thumbs, your knees, and anything else. Grim slabs are much like worming through a maze. The rock face is your maze. Oftentimes you can't see the barriers, but you'll feel them. If you lean in too far or over-grip too much, you'll slip off. If you lean too far back, your balance goes out of kilter and you skid off backwards.

Slab climbing requires maximum concentration, and will tax your mind to overload. Therefore, a relaxed mind is crucial. As with all forms of climbing, the idea is to climb using the least amount of strength. Climbing with this "light touch" is often the only way to succeed on difficult slabs, which require much more finesse than crimping might. Passing

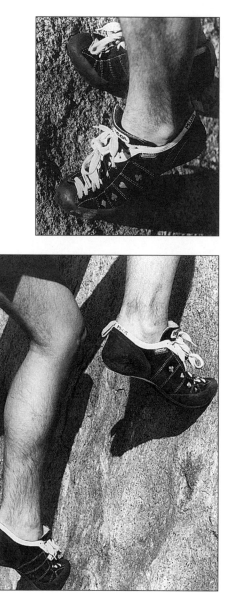

through sequences with the least possible effort requires, first and foremost, a focused mind. A tense mind produces a tense body, and a tense body only flounders on grim slabs.

With this relaxed mind comes an almost child-like trust, and the magic of finding yourself smoothly ascending, rather than quivering and shaking off your stances. Practicing games like chess are great for mental stamina and concentration. Practice on boulders. Your body knows what to do. Just allow yourself to move. Assess the moves, let your body soak up the information, relax, commit, and then go for it. Slab climbing isn't just for girls or those with broomstraw arms.

Slabs as Technique Builder

Slabs remain the best medium on which to hone general technique, particularly footwork. They also are excellent for mental conditioning. For the slab climber, good balance primarily is the result of assuming correct body position. On climbs that are less than vertical, get your boots to do the work. Use all your balance, mental muscle and patience. Fight the initial urge to hug the rock. That only directs your mass onto your boots at an oblique angle, forcing you to overcling with your hands in an attempt to compensate for the bogus balance and ever-slipping boots.

Smearing

Good smearing often is a matter of strong toes. Normally, you smear by lightly overlapping the hold with the boot's running edge. Since 1980, and the introduction of "sticky rubber" soles, many old edging problems now are readily smeared. No need to elaborate much here. The same techniques hold as with edging—shrewd choice of footholds, fluid weighting of the holds, and good body position only increase your smearing prowess.

Friction

The tires on a dragster are wide because the more rubber there is on the track, the better the "slicks" grab. Usually, the more of a boot's surface area you can apply to the rock, the better purchase you have. Note that as your heel rises and your weight moves onto your toes, less and less of the boot's sole remains in contact with the rock. Hence, you often will see climbers keeping their heels fairly low in an attempt to get a little more rubber onto the rock—just the opposite of the technique used on difficult edging. In addition, conscious pressing of the toes within the boot will force more toe rubber onto the rock.

For slab climbing, think about precision and economy of movement. And pay close attention to how you place your feet.

A little experience will tell you what works best, and where. It's mainly instinctual. Yet it's surprising how many climbers pay little attention to this all-important detail—precise footwork. More than a few climbers would be world-class, or damn close to it, if their footwork were just a little more precise.

Walking on Egg Shells

Extreme friction climbing resembles walking on egg shells—or trying to. The handholds are not there, so deft movement from one foothold to the next is crucial. In so doing, you are transferring all your weight onto what often are very marginal holds.

Where you place your foot is as important as how you place it. To a great extent, the able friction climber is the one who scours the face for footholds, then uses the best ones—with precision. The slightest roughness can make a huge difference in how well, or poorly, your boot will stick. So keep your eyes peeled for any sort of hold or irregularity, however marginal, and place that boot as the gem cutter strikes the ruby—precisely.

Maximize use of all footholds. The ability to do so is key to success on face climbs of all angles—from slabs to overhanging testpieces. Develop the knack to stand on the merest nothing as if it were a footstool.

Arm Position

Arm movement and position will be further taken up when we look specifically at vertical face climbing. For now, let's briefly review the basics.

Because slab and edging routes are lower-angled than other types of climbs, arm position is not so crucial in terms of saving strength. Most of your weight is over your feet, or should be. Arm position does affect your balance, however. The best posture is when your body is in a sort of relaxed X. That means both arms should be grabbing holds above your head. Obviously, the climb dictates exactly where your hands must go, and you'll routinely pull this way or that, with your hands to the side or even below your chest. Just remember that you are in better balance, and in a more natural posture to both stand and pull, when your hands are over your head and about shoulders' width apart. Strive to work with your arms in this position whenever possible.

Keep much of your focus on your foot placements.

Rules of the slab:

Use your feet precisely; maintain good body posture/balance; use your mind continually; relax and breathe; try not to fall; patiently climb through the maze.

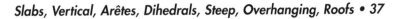

You'll sometimes see climbers who appear to be clinging to the rock for their lives, with their hands perpetually at chest- or shoulder-level—belt-level even. It's very hard to stay relaxed, in balance, and also avoid overclinging in this posture. Sometimes you need to assume a different position, for instance, if the holds are widely spaced—but among other drawbacks this blocks your downward vision, making it hard to zero-in on footholds.

HARROWING RUNOUT

The stamp of the classic slab and/or edging climb often is the shiver-me-timbers runout. Perhaps climbers traditionally have tried to run the rope on these routes because the falls are often—though not always—more skids than true plunges. Whatever the reasons, the technical rating of a slab or edging climb often is secondary to the relative protection of the lead—or the lack of protection, as it were. Mind you, all slab or edging climbs are not runout—not by any means. But there are more than a few that feature potential falls of 50 feet. On rare occasions, entire pitches have no protection whatsoever. Obviously, these climbs are not for everybody. They were designed for and are scaled by folk who climb for reasons other than mere "recreation." Anyway, since experienced climbers approach all runouts the same way—be the runout 10 or 50 feet in length—we can discuss things in general terms.

Shall I?

The first decision you must make is whether or not you're even interested in climbing a potentially dangerous route. And make no mistake about it—just because the route is not real steep does not mean a 25-foot fall, for instance, is harmless. Any fall can hurt you. If you decide to have a look at a runout climb, do so with an open mind. If you don't like the looks of it, don't let pride, or a pushy partner, commit you.

Once you reach the belay below the runout pitch, study the rock closely. If you decide to have a go, keep your options open. If you get to the runout and, for whatever reason, don't feel like casting off, just bail. There's always another day. If you still feel like having a go, think through the consequences. The tried-and-true method is to understand a simple formula entailing three key considerations: How long is the longest possible fall you can take? Estimate the potential and judge how far below the protection you will end up. Is the protection adequate to hold such a fall? And most importantly,

what, if anything, will you hit if you come off? Don't underestimate even the slightest feature. A small ripple or horn can catch an ankle and ruin your day. Know what and where any hazards are. Note that only the last of these queries is a true judgment call—will the protection hold? The length of the fall and the obstacles along the way can be visually determined. In a nutshell, answering these questions is the surest way to calculate the potential risk of any fall, regardless of whether the route is 5.0 or 5.14. If everything checks out, then you've got to put all doubts out of your mind and really go after it. Fear paralyzes power, saps resolve, and makes relaxing virtually impossible. If the potential fall does not appear to have dire consequences, but you're still petrified, it's better not to cast off.

Laird Davis on "Local Boys Do Good," Squamish.

Tad Craig photo

Unruffled

The key to climbing any runout is to stay calm and climb with absolute control. Try to stick with conservative, straightforward sequences, even if they require more strength to execute. Many legendary falls happen when the climber has a moment's lapse in concentration, tries a weird move, or gets rattled toward the end of the runout and simply defeats himself.

Not all runouts are hazardous—they have the potential, yes, but if you're a 5.8 climber and the runout is only 5.5, you've got it made if you can "keep the lid on."

The really risky runout is something all serious climbers will face somewhere, sometime. The possible scenarios are countless, but the bottom line is the same: You fall, you get hurt. Perhaps the protection is poor. Maybe there's no protection. There might be something to hit if you come off—like the ground. Whatever, the degree of risk is relative to how close the climbing is to your technical limit. If the climbing seems relatively easy, and you can keep your head together, the risks are usually, but not always, manageable. If, however, the long unprotected section is near your technical limit, you're playing with fire. There's a fine line separating the bold climber from the blockhead. Good judgement—which cannot be conveyed in a manual—is the call here. Just remember that few climbers get away with cheating injury for very long, and no climber gets away with it forever. Again, think hard before trying a route that is both difficult to protect and near your technical limit. Technical skill and placing protection are separate arts, and it's very questionable to push both points at the same time.

To reiterate...

- Maintain good body position.
- Use precise footwork.
- Keep a relaxed but steady pace.
- Scope the route and the topo prior to casting off.
- Develop a good strategy calculating runouts and potential falls.
- Avoid rope drag.

FALLING

Falling is an integral part of slab and edging routes. Many of these ascend featureless rock, but are bolt-protected, which eliminates—if the bolts are sound—much of the peril. On routes steeper than about 65°, the falling climber will almost certainly lose contact with the rock and go airborne. A slab fall, however, usually is more of a skid than a "wrencher." These factors all encourage a climber to challenge himself. Chance a fall if the consequences aren't too frightening, and don't ignore the consequences: How far can you fall? What will you hit? Will the pro hold the longest possible fall?

Knowing where you are in relation to your protection also is important. If you are directly above the pro, or nearly so, you should fall straight down and it should be uneventful if everything goes right—if the pro holds, if you hit nothing, and if you maintain correct body position. When you're off to one side of the protection—either directly to the side, as on a traverse, or above and to the side—things can get nasty in a hurry.

The most common injuries on slab falls are minor abrasions and barked hips and elbows. Because the rock is comparatively low-angled, your body naturally will grate over the surface unless you make a conscious effort to keep your torso away. Bruised hips occur when the climber gets turned sideways. Thus, there are two things to try to do. When you pop, keep both palms on the rock, arms bent but straight enough to keep your face and chest away from the rock. Keep your feet spread slightly apart and slide down on the soles of your boots. You want to slide down in a four-point stance, staying relaxed, and facing the rock. If you freeze up and get turned sideways, you can injure yourself quickly and unnecessarily. I've taken 50-foot falls in this posture and come away without a scratch. Doing so is, to a large degree, a result of pre-programming your mind. A fall happens so fast that, once airborne, you'll only have time to react. If you're pre-programmed to relax and assume the four-point stance, you're doing yourself a favor. If not, expect the worst. (But don't expect to see your life flash before your eyes. That's a load of crap.)

If you are off to one side of the protection, the main worry when falling is that you'll get jerked sideways and spin. This can twirl you like a rag doll, and you can smack limbs—perhaps even your head—on the rock (though a head/rock collision is rare). Again, you must maintain the four-point stance, trying to bridge, or skid, with at least one limb in the direction you are falling. If, say, you've traversed to the right, then try to absorb the spinning action with your left arm and leg. The right arm should be high and to the right, palming off the rock as you slide sideways, trying to maintain stability as you whip over. There is an art to this, much of which depends on natural agility. A few short falls can be very instructive. As long as you have the theory in your mind, you'll probably be able to perform it well enough. There's another method on traverse falls that is remarkably effective if you've the athletic ability to pull it off. It entails grabbing the rope just above your tie-in and sort of sprinting along the arc of your fall. This "Jack-be-nimble" method is not necessary on routes above, say, 70°, where it's easier to just slide across. But when the angle is just right, and the fall is a short one, it works well. Trip up and you're in trouble, however. ·

Constructive Fall

Many times a climber has fallen because he was so afraid of falling that he tensed up, climbed hesitantly, or made a hasty move that cost him. If the fall is uneventful, which it normally is, it can do wonders for a person's confidence. Knowing that short, well-protected falls can be harmless dispels the jitters and frees the climber to concentrate on the moves. You can rarely climb to your full potential if you are preoccupied with falling. You hear people saying that the only reason they managed the lead was because they were too scared to fall off. This is usually more of a "war story," than a true one, however.

Final note: Make sure that your rope is between your legs or off to the side, not tangled behind your leg, which can flip you upside down if you pitch off.

Jive Fall

Some climbers actually will jump off cruxes rather than try a difficult move that they think, correctly or not, they will fall off anyway. I suppose some fractured reasoning can justify this, but it seems like a self-cheat not to push yourself until you pop because of the difficulty. When you are climbing with a top rope, there is absolutely no reason not to climb until you fall off. Assuming you actually want to climb the pitch, it's really questionable not to give it an all-out try. How else will you ever learn your limit or improve?

Out Of The Blue

At least half of your falls will occur unexpectedly, usually when a foot pops off the hold. When you climb yourself into a position where you can't move on, warn your belayer. Then go ahead and try the move anyway. You might make it, and you're no worse off if you don't, unless, of course, it's a mantel.

After a fall of more than 20 feet, the rope suffers appreciable fiber elongation and structural deformation, most of which is recovered with time. So, after any longish fall, lower down to the belay, tie yourself in with a sling, and untie from the rope for at least 10 minutes (or switch rope ends). The knot absorbs upwards of 30% of the impact force, but will recover quickly once untied.

Lastly, all of these techniques have been mentioned to help reduce the chance of injury if and when you fall. Only a rascal would encourage someone to go fall off something. You never want to fall, no matter how harmless things may appear. But to always climb scared and never to push yourself for fear of falling is a very outdated approach to climbing. More conservative tactics once were essential—when hemp ropes routinely snapped and the pitons were malleable iron. Times have changed.

GAME PLAN

There is a procedure, or ritual, that good climbers go through before a lead. I'll repeat several previous notions, if only to drive them home. On difficult slab and/or edging routes, the protection often is thin and the potential falls often are long ones. So first, study the topo and make mental notes about how hard the route is, where the crux is, and anything else you can glean from the map. Bilk friends or acquaintances of all relevant info: get the "beta" if you're not concerned with getting the on-sight; otherwise scope the route, with your eyes and mind, as thoroughly as possible to gain maximum information available. Eyeball the devil out of the pitch in question and make certain what you see jives with the topo

and your friends' reports: Can you spot the roof, the horn, the tree? Where are the bolts, and above which one is the crux? Calculate the potential falls between protection, or where you imagine they would be should you have to protect the pitch yourself. Arrange your rack according to what the climb dictates. If you see you'll need runners straightaway, have them, or anything else needed, at the ready. Discuss things with your partner. In short, do a detective job from the deck, and get all your ducks in line before you cast off.

On the really bleak routes, consider these three, basic things: Focus, Form, and Rhythm.

Chris Goplerud falls from "Empty and Meaningless," Cochiti Mesa, NM.

Cameron M. Burns photo

Focus

Keen focus on the climbing at hand is essential because the holds often are hard to spot and correct sequences can be difficult to decipher. In a way, you can look at a difficult slab route as a complicated musical score that you must sight read and perform perfectly. You've got to stay focused throughout, and not let anything break your concentration. Master slab climber Rick Accomazzo was amazing at staying focused. Nothing could distract him, even the real prospect of a lengthy fall. The key is to realize and appreciate that your focus will increase relative to your confidence. Those first grim slabs will seem so slippery and insecure that you don't know what you can get away with, and the prospect of a fall looms so large that steady focus on the moves is impossible. In time, your ability to stay focused will increase as falling becomes less and less your primary concern.

The belayer must concentrate as well. He should keep a trained eye on the leader, feathering the line out, ever- ready to catch him should he pop. Sloppy belays can add yards to a fall simply because the belayer was caught unawares. Knowing that your belayer has all his attention focused on you helps free your mind to deal with the climbing, and is a real confidence builder when you've got to run the rope out a ways.

Form

No matter how grim the climbing gets, you should never abandon your form. If you ever have the chance to accompany a top climber up an extreme route, do it—even if you have to rest on the cord a few times. You don't want to make a career out of this, but everybody's done it at one time. Chances are the ace will fall a few times, if the route is a testpiece. You probably will be surprised by the fall, because it will come so unexpectedly. You'll be surprised because, right up until the ace pitched off, he never forsook his form. Trying wild, desperate moves is rarely, if ever, the solution to a difficult crux. Even if a dynamic move is required, control is the key.

When a climber confronts a climb that seems too difficult, the tendency is to start flailing. We've all seen this type of reaction in a boxing match. Often, the boxer is not even overmatched, but for whatever reason, he chucks form out the window and starts throwing haymakers. Rarely does such a blow find its mark. So, at all costs—even a fall—maintain your form. Relax, climb smoothly, and maintain control. Do not rush. If you can't do it with good form, how can you expect to do it with poor form?

Maintaining form is essential to make any real gains, particularly with climbers just coming into their own. It's an easy thing to think about, but most climbers consciously must try to maintain form until it becomes automatic.

Focus

Keep your thoughts on the climbing—nothing else.

Form

Never flail. Period.

Rhythm

Climb at the pace that allows you to maintain Focus and Form.

Rhythm

Setting a good pace is vital. The idea is to settle into a rhythm, into the flow, that is neither too fast, nor too slow. The climb and your aptitude (fitness, disposition, etc.) will in part dictate your pace, but remember this: Once you settle into a nice flow, you don't want to disrupt it with quick bursts or by "camping" too long, even on big footholds. Certainly, you should take advantage of rest holds, but don't stay so long as to fall out of sync, letting your focus lag, your muscles get cold, and your feet go numb. You're not in a track meet, but you're not up there to dink around, either. Get on with it in a measured, calculated way.

*Alex Russell stays
focused on "Scarface,"
14a, Smith Rock,
Oregon.*

Ian Yurdin photo

Power Rationing

In dealing with slabs and edging routes, we've talked about pacing, rhythm, and the necessity of climbing using the least effort. The need to husband your strength is even more important with vertical face climbing, principally because you rarely can get the kind of rest that allows you to recapture spent gas (more on this later on). The steeper the slab, the more vital it is to conserve power so your contact and calf strength are there when you most need them.

Common Mistakes in Slabbing and Edging:

- Not continuously scouring the face for best holds.

- Hugging, or laying against the rock (bad body position).

- Haphazard boot placement.

- Overloading boot with quick weight transfer, as opposed to smooth stepping onto footholds.

- Not keeping the boot still on the edge or allowing the boot to rotate on the edge once weighted.

- Overclinging with hands.

- Tensing up, climbing "frozen."

- Climbing "heavy" as opposed to cat-like.

- Climbing too fast, or too slow—bad pacing.

- Abandoning form.

- Failure to judge the consequences of a fall.

- Climbing with the hands too low and the feet too high.

- Too little attention paid to predicting probable sequences.

MODUS OPERANDI

We've gone over the ritual of studying the topo, then eyeballing the slab, recognizing and making mental notes about where the crux is, etc. Your gear is in order, and now you're set to cast off. How will you go about your business, and what you will have in mind as you climb over different sections? Here is one method that works well:

Say you are a solid 5.9 climber. The next pitch—your lead, incidentally—is rated 5.10–, but that's only the crux, which is short and near the end of the lead. The rest of the climbing is mostly 5.8. You know that everything but the crux is within your capabilities. So, in a sense, you can reduce the entire pitch to perhaps 10 feet of grim climbing, because that's how long the crux is. By looking at it this way, you shrink the questionable bit right down to size, and the project seems more reasonable. You also ease doubts and worries and can settle into a nice flow, getting your body and mind in a rhythm before you tackle the crux.

Make sure you don't race over the climbing before reaching the crux. Use the lead-up climbing to settle in and hit your groove. Conserve your gusto. That way you'll be ready when the going gets bleak. Once there, study the crux if you can, but not so long as to fall out of your groove.

Many slab/edging climbs are difficult not because of a certain hard crux, but because they are tiring and unrelenting. Known variously as "calf burners," "finger shredders," et al., they can be intense affairs because of the degree of concentration needed to assail them. Though these types of climbs might not have as high a rating as those featuring a vicious, overhanging crux, they often are just as challenging and almost always more work. An edging route rated 5.10a that features no climbing whatsoever under 5.9 is much more troublesome than a route rated 5.10d that is mostly 5.7, save for a couple beastly moves. That's why the ratings on slab and edging climbs can mislead us.

If the climb is continuously grim, bear these points in mind: Good concentration and continuous, fluid movement are essential. There is a tendency to both speed up and tense up as you near the end of the pitch. Avoid both by staying relaxed and focused. Settle in, stay cool and relaxed, and keep moving. Briefly rest at any decent hold. Stand on your heels and take a little pressure off your calves. Shake out your arms, relax your fingers. Then advise your belayer and have at it.

Arêtes

When two planes of rock converge to form a 90° corner, we have a textbook arête. In practice, however, arête-climbing occurs on any "edge" formed by converging faces. Generally, the sharper, more pronounced the edge, the trickier the climbing. Since the face-climbing revolution in the early '80s, climbers have gone crazy on arêtes, producing novel and technically-demanding routes up vertical—even overhanging —"outside corners." These routes offer some of the most dramatic climbing found cliffside, with the "double exposure" afforded by scaling the genuine edge compounding the intensity and splendor of the expedition.

Each arête requires something different from the climber whether straddling the edge itself, feet plastered high; changing sides several times in 10 feet; jack-knifing up both sides, hands clawing blindly around the corner; body-hinging; barn-dooring; heel-hooking to stay on. Often you end up with bizarre foot placements, like squatting on both feet. Yes sir, the possible sequences are infinite.

Arêtes present unique climbing problems. It's hard to directly contrast arête climbing with other modes of face climbing, and the person interested in becoming good at ascending arêtes should ease into the tournament. Most every crag presently has a slew of arête climbs. Start with the moderate ones, even if they're well below your normal standard. Becoming "arête fluent" comes most readily through repeating the unusual body positions, the various hooking (toe, heel, and calf) techniques and the strange and shifting balance problems. It's much like riding a bike—once you get the hang of it, you'll have the technique for life. Arête climbs almost always are exposed, committing, and exhilarating. Likewise, these routes provide some of the most spectacular falls you'd ever hope to see—or take. Because of the constant liebacking and counter-pressuring, a leader can rifle off like he's spring-loaded, and oftentimes he does so quite unexpectedly. Such peelers provide all the more reason to ease onto the moderate ones before pushing your luck on the desperates.

Stewart M. Green photo

On The Steep

It's a maxim for all forms of climbing that you keep your weight over your feet. It's crucial in friction climbing because often there are no handholds. To a great degree, the same goes with edging. With steep face climbing, our present focus, your arms will flame out unless your feet continually support your weight. The tendency is to yard primarily with

Arête sequence: good footwork is key!

the arms—and that is dead wrong. Never underestimate the value of any foothold, however skimpy. Even the slightest purchase with your feet makes a considerable difference. For example, if you can unweight yourself just slightly on a pull-up bar, perhaps by having a buddy tug on your belt loop, you can chin yourself another dozen times.

All the footwork tricks we've covered hold true with vertical face climbing as well. But now, everything's more strenuous, calf (edging) strength is all the more essential, and body position is different.

Suck It In

Once the angle of the rock reaches vertical, your torso will actually overhang your feet unless it is pasted against the stone. The more your torso is angled back beyond a vertical posture over your feet—the more you lean out—the harder it is to hang on. When you suck your body into the wall you are shifting weight off your arms and onto your boots. It's a good practice, but does not always mean the climb will be less strenuous on your arms.

We've already called the relaxed X body position the most natural and least strenuous. Same goes here. If your arms are somewhat extended to decent holds, sucking your torso into the wall does ease the strain because your weight is better situated over your shoes. But if the hands are positioned below the shoulders—even if they are latched onto good holds—it becomes very strenuous. Remember, the sharper the angle formed by your lower and upper arm, the more strenuous the position is. Conversely, the straighter your arms, the more bone structure (instead of contracted muscles)

To drive it home:

- Draw your body to the rock when the holds allow and the position feels natural.

- Keep your arms straight whenever possible—particularly when surveying the rock above—letting bones, not contracted muscles, bear the load.

- Once you have pulled yourself into a contracted position, arms bent and cranking, toes edging madly on holds, try to quickly extend into the relaxed X position.

can bear the load, resulting in a less strenuous posture. Of course, as you move upward and past holds, your arms become increasingly contracted. Avoid stopping in a compressed attitude. You don't want to hang out very long with your arms bent and your muscles contracting. Keep reaching above, to a side-pull or to any hold that will allow you to get your arms straight. Try and maintain long lines of limb, letting bone structure absorb the tension.

STATIC CLIMBING: VICIOUS CRANK

Vicious cranks usually are required to span long sections of rock between usable holds. This process involves several sequential phases: Crank/Step, Lock-off, Reach, Extend. You extend back into the relaxed X position, or an approximation of it, to get set-up to repeat the process. Each phase blends into the next, sometimes overlapping; but by breaking down the individual movements, we can better understand the centipede-like progression, as well as examine what can go right—or wrong—and begin making this knowledge an instinct.

Let's jump right into the middle of a hard crux section and look at the succession of movements:

(1) Set-up Phase

Your body is static—at least momentarily. You're standing on holds, legs somewhat extended, hands over your head or extended to the side. The boots bear maximum weight as you jockey your fingers around on the holds, getting set-up. However precarious the posture, you must try to relax here, to save strength and inhibit any wobbling on the holds. Acknowledge that whenever you've stopped, such as during this set-up phase, your toes will start to fatigue at a rate relative to how poor a hold you're standing on. If the holds are

minimal, it's essential to keep the boot's running edge firm and not hop around on the hold. Unless the foothold is a big one, move on before your tired calf forces movement on the hold. In extreme cases, when your feet are splayed onto weird slopers in unbalanced attitudes, each second's pause makes popping off more probable. It then becomes a feat of concentration to stay tight on the holds, however poor they may be. Also, it is during this set-up phase that you can most easily suck your hips and torso in close to the rock. This puts even more pressure on the feet, but they are better prepared to take the load than the arms. If you can shake out an arm here, do it, but quickly. (Up to 90% of your strength can be recovered in 45 seconds, but it takes many minutes, sometimes hours, to get back to 100%. And if you're really pumped, you'll have to wait a couple days to get it all back.)

Okay. Your lower body is perched on desperate turf to allow your hands the chance to get set-up for the ensuing crank. Simultaneously, your eyes are scanning the rock, reckoning the various sequence options overhead. Obviously, I can hardly second-guess the subsequent moves, but there are several things that can make your present, probably desperate posture, at least manageable.

As you set one hand, usually reaching the free hand high, the tendency is to overcling with the clasping hand. Be aware of this. If chalking up will increase your chances of pinging off, skip the chalk for that move. And watch your breathing. Don't hold your breath—that will only tense you up. Once your grip is set on the best available holds, you must quickly determine what holds you are pulling up to, and what footholds you will use. Do not simply start cranking, hoping you can reckon the next move once you're a little higher. The set-up phase is far and away the best time to try to reckon and visualize the following moves; so always strive to have a probable sequence in your head before pulling up.

(2) Crank/Step Phase

Because we're all quadrupeds, the crank/step phase is unavoidable and means most every sequence will require it in one form or another.

Starting this phase, the arms are extended and the hands are clasping edges. The next move is to place one or the other foot up to a higher edge, simultaneously crank with the arms, and step onto the edge. In so doing, we naturally move from the relaxed X position of the set-up phase into the collapsed X position. This phase, when executed, is what we refer to as "doing the move," though the start and finish to such a move or sequence is rarely so well-defined. The trick is to make sure one move is followed by another move.

First, the climb dictates what hold we're going to step onto. Make certain the boot is set ideally. Falls are most common in this phase, and usually result when the hastily-placed boot blows off the edge as we start weighting it. Hands blowing off holds is rarer, but still common. On truly bleak cruxes, climbers often fall mid-way through this crank/step phase. Either the foot has blown off, or they've bungled their positioning during the set-up phase, or the power just wasn't there to execute the crank.

When you start the actual crank, you want deliberate movement, not jerky, power-loading of either handholds or footholds, which probably are marginal anyway. Even when you are climbing semi-dynamically, you still want a fluid pull with the arms and a gingerly weighting of the foothold. Often, the hardest part of the crank simply is getting started, because it requires initiating a burst of power to the holds. Try to be fluid, rather than jerky or sudden, when you need to pour on the power. Once the arms are even slightly bent, it usually becomes much easier to crank. When starting the crank simply is impossible without a boost of some kind, consider a quick hip thrust, à la Elvis, which will push your torso closer to the wall and help get the crank started.

As you initiate the crank and step onto the higher foothold, the free foot ideally should move onto another edge as well. If that is unlikely, and the step is a high one, a little light paddling with the free foot can provide valuable upward body English. There is a subtle but very fundamental element of timing involved here, particularly if the move is so hard as to require explosive strength. This power timing—coordinating the limbs and hips in a quick, fluid, upward burst—is best understood and mastered on the boulders. Once you have cranked up, you've reached the next phase.

(3) Lock-off Phase

This is not really a phase, but it's worth studying because so many falls occur at this point. You're cranked up, probably on poor holds. Your leg is bent, boot edging madly on a hold—another bad one, most likely. You want to press out the foothold a bit more, get that leg straight or nearly straight, and get your weight on it. But before this is possible, you must get your hands well established on higher holds. You've pulled up on the present handholds, and soon will have to hang on one hold—locking your body off on it—while the free hand reaches for another hold. The key here is the lock-off on the clinging hand.

Rarely will handholds all be horizontal ones. Often, you're cranking on various side-pulls, pinches, etc. Regardless, the most secure position is when your elbow is drawn into your side: "elbow to lat," in parlance. Note that when you've

chinned yourself up on a bar and try to let go with one hand, still keeping your chin to the bar, you can do so only when your elbow is tucked to your lat (lat=latissimus dorsi muscle). Move your elbow out even slightly and you'll melt right off the bar. So when you have to let go with one hand and reach for a higher hold, always try to move your torso toward the locked-off hand, getting the elbow to your side. This works well even with side-pulls. Also, if you can splay your legs and draw your pelvis closer to the rock, it becomes less strenuous. This is not always possible, of course, particularly when balance is so critical that you can't juke your body without pitching off. A climber who has reached this impasse most often will slap for a higher hold, trying to snatch it before the clinging hand fades. Also, sometimes you will not be able to crank up high enough to get the elbow to the lat. In this case, try to get your near shoulder as close to the clasping hand as possible. This technique requires more strength, but is far more secure.

When the holds are too small or the position too tenuous to allow a lock-off, you are left to execute a "dead point," which will be explained later.

(4) Extension/Installation Phase

The installation phase takes you from the compressed and locked-off phase, to a phase where your posture is in some form of the relaxed X. In short, after you have locked-off, then reached for higher holds, you must extend far enough to install yourself back into the set-up position. (Note that virtually all moves go through this centipede-like progression—crank, step, lock-off, reach, extend—followed by setting up to repeat the process.)

Since your hands already are low, and you can't change the hold beneath your driving leg, you've got to install your hands on higher holds so you can press the leg out. If you're fortunate, you'll have two footholds, but it's uncanny how often you'll find that during the crank/step phase, you're pressing out a single foothold. Anyway, balance and strength are key here.

As you jockey your hands onto higher holds, pulling and extending into the set-up posture, the weight-bearing foot must remain exactly placed. If you've stayed on it through the crank/step phase, it probably won't blow if you can remain tight. The trick is to distribute your weight on a second foothold as soon as you are able.

Remember that you rarely can get a rest anywhere save in the relaxed X position of the set-up phase. Perhaps you can stop briefly in lock-off phase, if your foot is on a suitable hold, but maintaining this posture for long is usually more strenu-

(1) Set-Up Phase Objectives:

- Assume relaxed X position, or closest posture to it;
- Get hands extended onto best holds for the crank to follow;
- Reckon probable crank sequence;
- Chalk, if possible;
- Suck torso into rock, over feet, if possible.

Mistakes:

- Moving the boot, which pops off hold;
- Overclinging with hands;
- Pausing too long to chalk, if the holds don't allow;
- Choosing the wrong handholds for the following move;
- Not reckoning the next moves;
- Holding your breath and tensing up;
- Standing on one edge when another is available for free foot.

(2) Crank/Step Phase Objectives:

- Controlled upward movement;
- Selecting best foothold, placing boot precisely thereon and fluidly loading "stepping" foot, getting it to bear optimum weight;
- Remaining balanced despite the strain;
- Maintaining smooth power throughout the "crank."

Mistakes:

- Imprecise placement of "stepping" foot or excessive, jerky loading of foot which results in blowing off the hold;
- Getting stuck at mid-crank;
- Choosing the wrong handholds, which results in an undoable sequence.

(3) Lock-off Phase Objectives:

- Momentarily remain secure before reaching for higher handholds;
- Quickly survey and visually verify next move, or quickly revise "probable sequence";
- Set free foot on edge (if possible) to better distribute weight; maintain secure lock-off, keeping elbow to lat whenever possible.

Mistakes:

- Not cranking high enough;
- Not getting elbow to lat when possible;
- Not getting hips close to the rock;
- Letting the foot move on the edge and rotate off;
- Incorrectly reckoning next handholds.

(4) Installation Phase Objectives:

- Getting installed on next handholds (grabbing correct edge) and straightening out "pushing" leg;
- Extending into relaxed X posture;
- Getting both feet on best available holds.

Mistakes:

- Clinging hand melts off as free hand reaches;
- Free hand reaches for the wrong hold, loads it immediately, and you fall;
- Foot blows off hold as you fully extend leg;
- Free foot doesn't seek out edge.

ous than moving on. So as a general rule, we can say the faster you get installed into the set-up posture, back into the relaxed X position, the more energy you will save.

If you watch carefully how an expert climber moves, you'll see that there is a great economy of movement, combined with a near-constant flow. The only pause is at the set-up phase, which is the only place where you can judiciously stop, scan the next move, shake out and chalk up. The majority of rookie falls occur when the climber falls out of synch with the phases, and tries to either set up and/or pause in the middle of a move, or madly yards through when he should be setting up. You have to establish yourself on each hold you use, if only taking a fraction of a second to do so. Without this slight pause you've really no chance of using the hold in the best way.

Breaking things down into phases has simplified, perhaps oversimplified, vertical face climbing. Climbing sequences vary so much that they are difficult to discuss in any but the most generic terms. Still, we've discovered some truths, also generic, which will apply more often than not. Now it's time to look at those times when they will not.

DYNAMIC CLIMBING

The previous look at phases assumed that the climbing was controlled and static. However, as the angle steepens and the holds run thinner and farther apart, dynamic climbing increasingly comes into play. Many times, gently bounding over the difficulties is far less strenuous than slow, static movement. Let's look at the standard techniques.

Powerglide

Say you're in the set-up phase, in the relaxed X posture with legs extended, boots on holds, hands extended and clasping. The problem? The next handhold is way the hell up there. The handholds between your present position and the next are too scant to pull up and lock off; perhaps even if you did crank, step, and lock-off, your reach still would be shy of that next handhold. You might be able to span this stretch with a Herculean static move, but that would leave you so torched you couldn't carry on. You're looking, then, at a classic chance to "powerglide."

The powerglide is a controlled dynamic. You begin just as you would if you were initiating the crank/step phase. Once your hands are set, you toe a higher edge. If the foothold is in line with your body, it's straightforward to get some thrust off of it. If you have to stem a foot out to the side, the physics are all wrong for upward drive, and the foothold is of negligible value. You do not simply throw yourself upward off marginal handholds with no consideration of the foothold. If anything, the foothold is more crucial than the handholds. Anyway, once the foot is placed on the higher edge, you must generate sufficient thrust—by yanking with the hands, keeping the

The powerglide

hips in and quickly extending off the foothold—that your vector will carry you past the lock-off point and to within slapping range of the higher handhold. In other words, you "powerglide" to that next hold.

Make certain the boot is placed precisely on the edge. Almost all of the time the extending leg provides the upward thrust; the hands only initiate the glide (also keeping your torso close to the rock). When your leg extends, the boot's edge must maintain accelerating mass well beyond your actual weight. The edge will blow off unless it is precisely placed, and the attitude and positioning of the toes must remain constant. Remember, maintaining contact with the rock means maintaining control. In maximum powergliding, you might actually have to toe high off the hold, stretching your heel way up for that added inch—but your boot must never become dislodged from the hold. You never actually jump off the edge unless you're going a mighty long ways, and the sought-after handhold is sufficient to support all of your body weight on its own. In other words, leaving the rock completely in a desperate reach for a handhold is virtually impossible to execute successfully unless you're gliding for a plentiful hold, like a jug. Gliding around off little tweakers is reserved for Captain Granitic. Let's go through the motions:

You're set up, hands and feet on holds, poised. You spot the high handhold a ways above, and decide to powerglide to it. You surgically place your boot on a higher hold, which must be good enough to bear the thrusting leg. (Better an edge, even a small one, than a smear.) Then, you lock your eyes back onto that higher hold as a Zen archer would draw a bead on his target, a solitary grain of brown rice. In one coordinated burst, keeping your hips in, you heave with the hands, and as your weight comes onto the foothold, you quickly but fluidly extend your leg, pushing your body into dynamic motion, powergliding up. As you glide past where you'd normally lock off, your hand keeps clasping hard, pulling strong.

Slap it!

How soon you release a free hand to slap for the higher hand-hold depends how good, or poor, the clasped holds are. There are many degrees of powergliding. Skilled climbers often powerglide all over a pitch, avoiding more strenuous static moves. In a situation where all holds are ample— the thrusting foothold, the pulling handhold, and the hold the climber's gliding for—he can avoid a grievous lock-off and simply powerglide to the next hold, nice and easy-like, executing more of a quick reach and latch than an all-out slap. If the handholds are bleak, however, a climber should wait until he's reached the top of his glide, then quickly slap for the hold. Like a fly ball, the climber is momentarily weightless at the apex of the glide—the dead point—and that's when you release a hand and slap for the next hold.

Latch it!

Remember three things about this stage of the dynamo. First, the slapped hand must hit the hold exactly: it must be a bull's-eye. Second, the fingers most often should land in the open grip configuration. Third, try to generate enough height with the glide that you're not latching with a fully extended arm. If the arm is slightly bent, the muscles are set to exert the necessary clinging power. Overshooting is possible, but more likely on all-out dynamos.

The powerglide is a standard face-climbing technique, requiring precise timing, coordination, considerable contact and explosive strength, and a certain natural athleticism. The technique most readily is mastered on boulders. Learning the intricacies of dynamic climbing on the lead is like learning to drive by racing the Indianapolis 500—not a sound plan.

A lesser, more delicate form of the powerglide—the dead point—will be taken up in detail shortly. For now, understand that this "dead point" refers to that split-second when the climber is weightless, at the apex of a lunge, when he is neither going up nor down. Though describing this moment of weightlessness, dead point also refers to a form of dynamic move. Rather than propelling your body upwards, the dead point usually involves dynamically drawing your body into the rock— usually vertical or overhanging rock—and at the "dead point," flashing a hand up for a higher hold. In the following chapters we will hear plenty more about this important technique.

Side-glide

Occasionally, it is necessary to chuck a lateral dynamic. The process does not significantly differ from vertical power gliding. If you're required to cover a pretty good stretch, it's almost always a matter of dynamically rocking over onto a foothold and either semi-falling, or flinging yourself sideways. Whether falling or flinging, you're not going to be successful without a workable foothold. Oftentimes, said hold will slope in the direction of thrust. Success depends on the aforementioned factors, but it is even more crucial with side-gliding that the prospective handhold be a good one, preferably slanting your way. To help keep your swing in check, it sometimes helps to drag your boot rand or toe across the rock as you glide. If you're thinking of side-gliding way to the flanks, hoping to stick a poor hold that slopes away from you, you'd better have a hardy belay and a bolt at your waist.

FULL-BLOWN DYNAMIC

A full-blown dyno roughly can be described as requiring part, if not all, of the body to become totally dislocated from the rock during the upward flight. A truly world-class dislocate dyno is perhaps the most outrageous, and rarest, move in climbing. Its execution greatly favors a muscular climber who can generate the requisite explosive boost, combining enough spring to slam-dunk a basketball with enough hoist to hurl himself up and off a pull-up bar. Because so few climbers can do either, most dislocate dynos are well below world-class length. World-class dead point and powerglide dynos are required on most genuine testpieces.

Heidi Badaracco power-gliding at Sinks Canyon, Lander, Wyoming.

Beth Wald photo

World-class dislocate dynos are found almost exclusively on boulders, and their utility for sportclimbing generally is overstated. For instance, the Left Eliminator at Fort Collins, Colorado, is one of America's most famous boulder problems. It's considerably shorter than world-class length and first was done 30 years ago, yet the number of climbers who have bagged it on their first try can be counted on one hand—and many of America's best have tried. The point is, few if any climbs require the world-class dislocate dyno since so few people actually can do them. Still, dislocate dynos are becoming more common on overhanging routes, so it's worth our while to understand the fundamentals.

The Dangler

The most strenuous dynamic is the one started with the feet already dangling. Say you're hanging on the lip of a roof and the next hold is a knob three feet above you. You can't mantel on the lip; your only hope is to fire for the knob. That means you must generate enough boost to hurl yourself three feet straight up. Anyone would be hard-pressed to do so using only his arms. The trick is to bring the lower body into play.

The standard technique is this: Get your hands situated on those spots from which you can generate the best hoist. Hanging from straight arms, gently swing the lower body in and out. When the feet swing out perhaps two feet past vertical, or whatever feels right, it's time to fire. Remember that as you swing, the torque on your hands changes. The more you swing out, the less secure your grip is, so you don't want to swing more than is necessary. In short, as the legs swing inward, prepare yourself. As they start to swing back out, start to initiate the hoist with the arms, simultaneously using the momentum of the swinging legs to aid the upward movement. On longish dynamos you may even draw your legs up and immediately extend them again in a controlled little kicking move (in gymnastics, this is called "kipping"). It's all a matter of momentum and timing. Once you start to fly up, the common mistake is to stop yarding with the arms. This can leave you short of the mark. Keep cranking, and even at the dead point, when your free hand lets go to flash up for that knob—particularly at this point—keep trying to chuck that handhold to the ground. Keeping constant power on the initial holds (power point) means when you do latch that knob, you won't have to shockload it because you stopped cranking on the lower holds.

Everything previously mentioned about dynamics applies here as well. Try to get sufficient height to hit the hold with a slightly bent arm, since the muscles already are kicked in, then hit the hold with a ready grip, not just a slapdash hand. Precise timing on when to flash the hand up at your dead point is essential. As mentioned, some people find that by dropping the head it is easier to generate good air. This means as you fly upward, you must glance quickly up, lock your eyes onto the hold, and hit it perfectly with the reaching hand. Personally, I always try to keep a good bead on the lunged-for hold, finding it easier to hit a bull's-eye when I'm looking at it. If there's a decrease in hoisting power by keeping my head upright, I simply kip and yank a little harder. How and when you look at the goal is a matter of personal preference. Note that many pitchers glance away just before throwing home the pitch, and they don't seem to throw more than the usual number of bean balls.

Double Mo

Far and away the most outrageous move in climbing—and the most infrequently used—is the two-handed dynamic dislocate. This is truly throwing yourself from one hold to another, so that at one point the body loses contact with the rock altogether.

The double mo rarely is used unless the thrust holds are good ones, and the lunged-for holds, or hold, is so poor that you cannot hang onto it with only one arm. In extremely rare situations, the two-handed mo is the only way to span a huge section of rock—say four feet across. Here, both the thrust and lunged-for holds must be good ones. Only two times in 25 years of climbing have I had to use this technique on an actual route, and they were the most spectacular moves I've ever done. The double mo is a game of power and timing. We've all seen the female gymnasts flying between the uneven parallel bars. They accomplish this by generating momentum off the lower bar (the power point), and heaving on it until their shoulders are well above it. The trick that makes this rock move different from other forms of dynamics is that you must release the power point before you reach the dead point. That is, you unlatch and swoop both arms up while you are still accelerating up. The goal is for both hands to latch the higher hold at your dead point. Timing and accuracy must be perfect. And both arms must be pre-cocked so you can cling like a gila the moment you hit that upper hold. Best to experiment on boulders. Too much theoretical talk can only confuse the issue. It's pretty sketchy to try this technique on a route before you've mastered, or at least are familiar with, its nuances. It's definitely the hardest technique in climbing. But, since the two-handed mo is so infrequently used, it's more of a novelty than a practical skill. It's certainly fun to know how to do, though. To see someone uncork a really long two-hander is pretty amazing viewing.

Didier Raboutou at Rifle, Colorado.

Beth Wald photo

Overhanging Face

By now you should well understand the basic tenets of face climbing: maintaining shrewd body position and a relaxed bearing; using precise placement of hands and feet while conserving energy and climbing aggressively over crux sections; remembering to always look ahead and plan your ascent. These notions all directly apply to overhanging face climbing. However, as the rock steepens, gravity changes the physics involved, and one's body position must respond and adjust to factors unique to overhanging rock. The technique of pulling up on holds, as well as the consequent arm and lower torso position, varies from that used on vertical terrain. Because overhanging routes are often more strenuous than vertical climbs of even the same rating, technical adjustments generally are aimed at conserving strength.

Hinge It

Check out any playground where kids swing on the jungle gym. Note how they can stay on the bars for a very long time. Note also that their arms are like broom straws, and you'll realize that it's not just muscular strength that's keeping them up there. Finally, note that they always hang and swing from straight arms. They simply don't have the power to start locking the bar off—never mind chinning themselves on it. These kids use two vital skills that apply to climbing overhanging rock: Try to always keep your arms straight, and consider your shoulders a hinge.

As mentioned a dozen times, you should keep your arms straight whenever possible, for it allows the bones, rather than constricted muscles, to bear much of the weight. But even arrow-straight limbs cannot keep your forearms from burning when they are working overtime to keep the fingers clasping the holds. With proper conditioning, the forearms can manage

the stress. The back muscles, though, require enormous energy, of which even the best climber has a limited amount, to pull up and lock off a hold on overhanging terrain. Because most overhanging routes require you to pull up and lock off somewhere—if not many times—you'll want to conserve the back muscles by trying to climb with straight arms whenever possible. That way, when the lock-off comes, you'll have the gas to perform it. Learning to use your shoulders as a hinge, while letting your driving legs provide the upward thrust, is the trick to keeping the arms straight while continuing upward movement.

Annie Whitehouse at Red Rocks, Nevada.

Beth Wald photo

Both the concept and the mechanics are basic. Your hands clasp holds, and straight arms lead back to your shoulders. As the legs fluidly push off footholds, the torso levers up with the shoulders as the hinge point. If you visualize this, you'll see that the farther you push/hinge your torso out with your feet, the farther your head moves out from under your hands. On extremely overhanging routes, like roofs, it feels somewhat natural to have your head directly below your hands, in line with straight arms, as gravity dictates. When you thrust out with your legs, however, you're pushing your head past the natural gravity point. While this saves the back muscles, it stresses the forearms in proportion to how far your head goes past the gravity point, or how far you hinge out. Ideally, you'll want to reach for a higher hold close to the time when your torso reaches the gravity point. When you pass that point, you'll either have to suck in and lock off, then reach, or perform a quasi-dynamic little hinge swing to reach that upper hold.

FOOTWORK

Your feet perform two essential functions on overhanging rock: supporting your lower torso and providing push for upward movement. If your feet are not placed properly or hooked on something, you'll be left hanging entirely from your arms—the worst position on an overhanging route because your arms will burn out in a matter of yards, period. Most of the time, you should strive to look for and utilize a combination of both hooks and pushing footholds. First, let's talk about the hooks.

There will be places for your feet, though you'll have to work at finding the most secure spots. Let's start with the really overhanging stuff—routes steeper than 120°.

Because much of your body is back and under your hands, gravity wants to peel your feet off any hold and leave you hanging straight up and down, directly under your beleaguered arms. Consequently, there always is a constant pull on your feet, as though weights were attached to your heels. Simply placing your foot on a good edge does not always work well. On routes that are just over vertical, this is not so much a problem. But once the angle really starts to kick back, you must try to get your foot lodged, or hooked, on or between holds.

Captain Hook

The standard hook is the heel and toe variety. The exact positioning depends entirely on the available hold. On a bucket edge, say, one commonly uses the very end of the heel. On smaller holds, you will have to jockey the heel around and use whatever part bites best. Whatever the position, you'll want to both drape the heel on the hold and apply a little downward pressure to keep the heel well-seated. The more your leg is bent, the more pressure you'll want to apply. Once the leg is extended, sufficient downward pressure occurs naturally as gravity attempts to rip your heel off the hold. Remember that the rand, the heel cup, or any of the ancillary rubber on the upper part of the boot is usually of the same "sticky" stuff that the sole is made of. Try to get some of this tacky matter on the hook, whatever the foot's position on the hold.

Insecure heel and foot hooks call for ingenuity on the part of the climber. Lodge it, jam it, hook it on the rand, pry it with the toes, but by all means, get that foot hooked on something. Sometimes a good hold is facing the wrong way—away from you. If you can get one foot in a position to push, you often can snag the other toe on the away-facing hold, and pull with it. The opposing pressure between the two feet will help keep your torso locked in, and is an excellent, useful technique on steep terrain.

LEGENDARY ABS

Legendary abdominals are but one step beneath titanium abs. And believe it—you'll greatly benefit from a set on overhanging terrain. Since your torso hinges at the waist and is never connected to the rock, the abs are the bridge between your points of contact; i.e., your hands and feet. They keep your torso straight when required, and are remarkably taxed when doing so. There is no mystery to getting legendary abs—all it takes is hard work. (Remember that incline sit-ups tend to work only the upper ab. Leg and knee raises hit the lower abs, which take much of the stress in truly overhanging climbing.)

Many sequences require legendary abs. One of the most common, and strenuous, involves using both hooks and thrusting holds for the feet. Say your hands are set and you're eyeballing the next holds. One foot is hooked, the other ready to thrust. As you thrust with the leg and pull/hinge with the arms and shoulders, often you'll have to free the hooked foot to get enough height to reach the next handhold. Here you must simultaneously release the hook and thrust off the foot, hinging off the shoulder. Next, you must let go with one hand and reach above. For a moment, you're hanging on only one arm, with your thrusting foot pasted on a hold without the stabilizing hook. This is where the legendary abs must kick in, keeping the torso tight until you can get set up on the higher holds. You'll often see a climber simply collapse at the middle and sag off the rock. Whenever you can keep the hook while thrusting for higher holds, make certain to do so. It's the much more secure technique, even if it's not always possible. The aim is to let those legendary abs hold you in check until you can get established on the next holds, where you can secure another hook to ease the load.

Bobbi Bensman in the Flatirons of Colorado.

Beth Wald photo

HANDS

Hands, arms, shoulder movement, and body position all blend into one equation on overhanging climbs. The climb dictates what handholds you use, and most climbers differ on preferred grips: some prefer to crimp the holds; others (now the majority) favor an open grip. The actual hold usually dictates one grip over another. When you've a choice, the type of grip used often depends on strength. One usually can apply more crank using a crimp, but this grip is far more troublesome on your joints.

While the open grip requires more sheer contact strength, and may feel less secure than the crimp, it oftentimes is your only choice. There is little to be said about the slew of other possible grips—pocket grips, pinches, etc.—save that the more you use your thumb, the more secure you probably will be.

Hand Position

Ideal hand position means the hands are never placed wider than the shoulders. Imagine that your shoulders form a boundary extending in to the rock. Whenever you reach out-

side this boundary, the climbing becomes far more strenuous. Normally, the upper torso follows the hands, falling in line directly below them. Whenever you use holds that are widely spaced—if the holds are anything shy of buckets—the physics of the operation means your shoulders must crank overtime to accomplish the move. Since you are often required to reach outside this imaginary box, build your shoulders up through loads of climbing and weight training. The result is an enviable corpus and boni fide cranking ability. Must haves.

Lock

We have gone over the notion of hinging off the shoulder while pushing off a foothold or hook. Though hinging is the preferred, strength-saving technique, it is limited by the fact that hinging with straight arms narrows your reach. Sometimes (or oftentimes, depending on the route) you must crank your torso up into the wall, lock off, then reach. The same rule that applies to all lock-off moves also applies here: Get the elbow to the lat. The lock-off becomes less viable and possible once the angle nears a flat out roof. Here you usually must hinge/swing between holds.

Sideways

A lock-off on overhanging terrain means gravity will try to turn you sideways. Don't fight this tendency. Allow your body to twist slightly, letting the outside shoulder dip away from the inside, pulling hand. This is a much more natural position, and it's a far less strenuous method to get that elbow to your lat.

Ron Kauk on "Supersonic," 13b, Tuolumne, California.

Beth Wald photo

Trying to keep your chest parallel to the rock face when locking off requires far too much strength, and is inefficient and out-of-balance. Most body juking and torso twisting is aimed at finding a more natural posture. Finding that position helps you find the place where you can best use your lat muscles.

Lead for Safety

On steep, extremely overhanging sport routes (one pitch or less), most climbers prefer to lead, for several reasons: If you fall off on top rope, you may not get back to the rock; if you can get reattached on the stone, it's often beastly strenuous climb back into the sequence once you've pitched off and lost the flow. Better to lead and bounce if you have to. If falls are inevitable, practice "soft" belays, where you have some slack in the line as you catch the falling climber. Don't suck in the rope, which makes for a hard fall sometimes causing injury. Most sport climbs are so well protected that a fall beyond ten or twelve feet is rare. Because so little rope is out (especially early on in the lead), short falls can't fully exploit the dynamic qualities (the rope's capacity to stretch) of the cord, and the fall is something of a "wrencher." A little slack—read "little"— in the rope can ease the wrenching effect of short falls. On roof climbs this is not so much of a problem. On lesser-angled routes, a wrencher can jerk a leader around like a rag doll, and slam limbs into the rock. The idea of a soft belay is to let the leader fall a foot or so farther, while providing smoother deceleration. This should only be done when there is no potential of hitting the ground. Take major precautions when refining this technique.

FALLING

When you pitch off an overhanging route, you drop like a stone. Unless you're climbing a genuine roof, you run the very real risk of swinging back into the wall and smacking it. Accordingly, and especially on routes in the 110° range, once you go airborne you immediately must get braced for impact. The technique is basic and needs no exhaustive study. Get your feet out. You don't want to lead with your head. Juke your body around so you swing into the wall straight-on, hitting it feet-first with the legs slightly bent and ready to absorb the jolt, like shock absorbers. Whatever you do, do not start flailing, pawing the air and screaming like a banshee. Appraise the fall before you commit yourself to the climb, and be prepared if the fall comes. Provided your ropework is in order, keeping your head together is your best insurance against injury.

There is the chance your foot will get entangled in the line. If that happens during a fall, you'll get twirled around or hung upside down. It's a function of how your weight impacts the pro. Always be aware of where the rope is running as you climb. Try to keep it between your legs, never allowing it to run on top of your leg or around your side.

Them Legs

In review: On overhanging routes and roof climbs, the legs play a crucial part. The more you use your legs in weird stems, with heel hooks, toe hooks, knee locks, body "scubbing"—all those places where legendary abs act like your glue—the easier time you will have passing through steep and horizontal madness. Maintaining a strong connection (again, legendary abs) between your legs and arms is what core strength is all about, and is vital for burling out steep terrain. Shoulder strength is likewise key, as well as the ability to climb when outrageously pumped. It's mind-bending, strenuous work, but remarkably fun.

Cut Loose

The most secure knee lock or heel hook must be forsaken when it's time to push on and reposition your foot. The trick is to try and move from a secure position to an insecure one and still maintain body control—impossible without strong abs. Your feet may cut loose momentarily; if so, try and reposition your feet back on the rock ASAP. Occasionally, it is easier to climb briefly with your feet free-hanging, but generally you'll want to use all fours.

Sometimes, rather than forcing your feet onto the rock, it's better to counter balance with a leg dangling out in space.

When appropriate, this technique can relieve considerable stress from your guns. If you try and force both feet in an awkward position, one foot might be good, but setting both on a tight spot is often more arduous and compromises the one good foot. Because you have two feet doesn't mean you always have to put equal pressure on them. The thin air may be the best "foothold" for a particular move; but as soon as you can effectively set both feet back on the wall, do so. Typically you dangle a foot or leg when the going is very steep and crunchy; as you proceed onto the next move, you may find it best to switch your foot out and replace it with the dangling limb. Turning the lip of a roof is often bizarrely strenuous. Remember that you're heading onto lower-angled terrain, often vertical or less. So as your hands reach around the lip, take heart that the angle is lessening.

Brett Spencer-Green on "Sneak Preview," Dinosaur Mountain, Boulder, Colorado.

Stewart M. Green photo

Bouncing Up

As mentioned, it's usually safer to lead, rather than follow, steep climbs, since a fall will be into the air, rather than onto the rock. That's why on many one-pitch sport climbs you'll see a team taking turns leading: One leads, the other belays. Once the lead is done, the leader lowers/raps off, pulls the rope, and the climbers exchange positions.

On super steep routes, once you've fallen off and are dangling in the air, you'll have to bounce to get back onto the rock, or else lower off and start from the ground. Bouncing is like doing pull-ups on the rope: As you bounce down, you'll shortly run out of stretch in the rope and will recoil back up. For a split second, you are weightless, and it is then that your belayer must suck in rope. Another technique that works in concert with bouncing is for the dangling leader to yard himself up by grabbing the rope, and then letting go. The trick is for the belayer to suck in some little rope before the leader bottoms out again. You'll be lucky to get a foot of gain for each pull up, but there's really no other way. These techniques work very effectively, but require perfect timing with your belayer. It also requires patience and burl. It can smart your hands, and you'll need to rest when you finally make it to the rock because you'll be hosed from pulling up so much. It's all part of roof duty.

FLASH IT!

Says "Cocoa" Joe Sloan: "The best way to climb anything is to walk up to it, draw a breath, and solo the bastard." Coarsely put, but there's no arguing Joe's point. If everyone knew they would never fall, no one would ever use a rope. The next best thing to soloing is an on-sight ascent—climbing the route, no falls, no beta, on your first try—which amounts to essentially the same thing as Joe's method. You've simply used gear, just in case you fall.

To scale a route on your first try, study the topo, scope the route from below and incorporate everything you know about climbing and are about to find out. (If you're not interested in on-sighting the route and prefer to attempt a flash ascent, ask for beta). At first glance, most steep and/or overhanging climbs look impossibly hard. Your eye also tends to exaggerate the angle, whereas the entire climb looks like a wave crashing on you. In fact, most steep/overhanging routes feature at least some vertical sections. Visually inspect these spots and, once on the lead, take advantage of them.

Strategy

It cannot be overstated: Success on difficult routes requires you to maintain focus, form, concentration, technique, rhythm and pacing. Regardless of a climb's numerical rating, most every steep face route involves stringing moves together between good holds. "Good" holds will, or should, dictate your pace— how fast you climb between the good holds, and, once gained, how long you stay at them. It's almost always better to try and de-pump by standing on these "good" holds, rather than by hanging off them and trying to shake out one arm at a time. Regardless, you should always scout the pitch from below, and know where any good holds are, or appear to be. This helps you formulate a probable strategy. Remember, however, that more than one plan has been abandoned upon discovering that what looked "bomber" from below turned out to be a glazed bowling ball once clasped. Always be open to anything and everything.

My strategy here is again to break the route into various sections—this time between "good" holds. A common mistake is to devise a strategy based on where the bolts or protection are. Although it should, not always does a bolt signify a break in the action. Also, you never know who placed the bolts—it could have been a climber with no concept of position, or it could have been someone who thoughtfully installed the bolts to facilitate easy, or at least possible, clips. Since virtually all clip-and-go routes are at least adequately protected, injury rarely is the problem. Climbing them is. That's why, generally, climbers map out a strategy according to where the good holds are, and consider a grim clip part of the overall sequence.

The idea is simple: Reduce the route to sections between good holds, then start estimating where the most strenuous bits will be. That done, factor in the location of the crux. Now you can estimate what parts will require the most effort, where you should try and cop a decent rest, and how fast or slow you should move over given sections. Once you have the route cased, you are free, and advised, to deal with one section at a time. This approach gives you an idea of what to expect, and can positively affect your overall success. It does not, however, help you overcome individual moves.

Grim Sections

There are two aspects to climbing hard sections: predicting the best sequence, then doing it. Face climbs often are spangled with chalk marks. These help to identify holds, but also mislead because they don't tell you which holds are useful, and which are useless. Remember, chalk marks tell a story, but the tale is a confusing one. The real value of chalk marks is in delineating a hold that you might not have seen otherwise. Whether that hold is of any value is your call. You may find that the hold of choice— for you—is completely unchalked. That is a brilliant discovery, to find and use what no one else has likely used, but what proves to work best for you. Such is the beauty of being open to all possibilities and not pigeon-holing yourself into only "following the chalk/ chalked holds."

Watching your partner (or anyone) do a sequence is instructional, but you can run into problems when trying to duplicate another climber's moves down to the smallest nuance. A person's strengths, technique, dimensions, and flexibility can mean that what was easy for he might be impossible for thee. Everyone must discover their own best way.

An example: For several years, I did most of my free climbing with Lynn Hill, who certainly is one of the world's great climbers. She could splay her legs out like Olga Korbut, do magical things while being absolutely balled up, had the kind of balance and staying power I could only dream about, and seemed fearless of any potential fall. I had a little more experience, a tad more explosive strength, a 12-inch reach advantage and about 100 additional pounds to haul around. We could rarely do things as the other had, and attempts to do so were frustrating for each of us. Often, we climbed the same route in completely different manners. Only a few times could she not climb something I could, and then only because the one and only hold simply was beyond her reach. Otherwise, she floated up everything I did—and more than a few I couldn't—often in the lead, and often with far greater ease than I had. The same thinking applies to "betas."

Pace It

The most important consideration, one that absolutely can be decisive on overhanging routes, is pace. No matter what your level, once you have acquired suave technique, the moment you start approaching your technical boundary, the limiting factor is strength. For everyone. What makes overhanging climbing unique among sports (and tricky to understand) is that two different types of strength are required. Obviously, you need good endurance, or staying power, to make it up an overhanging route of any length. But good staying power alone won't get you over the crux—you need explosive strength for that. However, you have only a limited amount of explosive strength, and once you use it, your staying power is greatly reduced.

Though the correlation is an inexact one, let's look at another sport to try and understand this complex notion. In long-distance kayak racing, the strategy is to never go so fast that you go "anaerobic." Simplified, anaerobic is the state in which your body uses more oxygen than you can suck into your lungs. Once you get that paddle moving like a bee's wing, you quickly go into this oxygen-debt state and the only way to recover is to stop, or to paddle so slowly that you'll see nothing but the other competitor's backs for the duration of the race. In a long race, you'll often see the leader put on short bursts in an attempt to get those trailing to paddle so hard that they'll go anaerobic trying to catch up. Those that fall victim to this strategy essentially eliminate themselves from the race. With overhanging climbing, the same kind of fizz-out can occur. The harder you work on the easier sections, the less explosive strength you'll have, and once you tap heavily into your explosive strength, your staying power is so reduced that you'll have to contrive a rest or you'll quickly burn out and pitch off. Consequently, it is essential to use the least amount of strength on each section. You never want

Mia Axon on "Sneak
Preview," 11d,
Dinosaur Mountain,
Boulder, Colorado.

Stewart M. Green photo

to power over a section if you can ease your way over it using
heel hooks and straight arms. You want to climb at a pace that
requires minimum effort: quickly here, slowly there, resting
here, etc. Pace, then, is all about conserving both your
endurance and explosive strength.

Rest Stop

Knowing when to rest and when to carry on is crucial. Much
of this comes from your ability to read your own body, from
knowing its capabilities and limitations. When you can stick
an entire leg into a hole and let go with both hands, obviously you can stop and rest. But the game is rarely that black and
white. Often you have to fiddle around to find a rest, and the
more convoluted the rock, the more convoluted the rest
stance will be. Ledgeless, overhanging limestone like the
stuff in Rifle Mountain Park, Colorado, for example, might at
first glance seem to offer scarcely a shake-out, let alone a
hands-down snooze. Yet the discerning eye can find a rest on
most any wall, regardless of the holds or angle. As you climb,

and before you get pumped, look around—that two-foot roof you're cranking now might offer a solid knee-bar underneath. Knee-bars are the perfect rests, but arm-bars can be life-savers as well. Look for these anywhere a knee-bar might go— deep scallops, shallow cracks, in between blocks, under roofs. In some instances you might even rest by cocking your head under an overlap or simply draping your forearms over a flat shelf. A fist jam is also a useful—and often overlooked—rest on many face climbs. The route you're on may not have a crack, but a good fist (or hand) jam doesn't necessarily need one. Limestone stalactites, conglomerate knobs, and pock-ets, all offer jamming possibilities. Be creative. And while cop-ping a rest, don't just let your arms hang like bratwursts. Swing them around, massage them, beat those forearms against the rock, and flex those fingers. All these efforts will drive fresh blood into your goosed arms, giving you a shot at the tweaker crux above.

No Rest

If there is no rest and you're getting pumped, get on the best holds available, but hang from them using your ring and pinky fingers. Sacrificing those fingers, while still taxing, will partly rest your "main pullers," the index and middle fingers and thumb. Alternately, laying the meat of your palm along large edges or knobs will give your fingers a respite. Along the same line, if you know that the crux above demands a low lock-off from your right arm, then find a large hold and hang from your left arm until you're reasonably sure your right arm has had enough rest to pull the crux move.

But before you start any rest, you must ask yourself some questions: Will stopping at this particular hold result in recov-ery or even greater fatigue? Are you actually making the climb harder by trying to stop? Will you have enough gas to climb the crux if you don't stop and shake out somewhere soon? These questions, and a dozen more, must be answered on each overhanging route— when to climb fast, when to pause and study the rock overhead, when to speed over a stretch, when to chalk, and when to stop altogether. Once the climbing gets bleak, you rarely have the option of stopping at all. All concentration must be focused on climbing the route. You either make it, get stumped by a move and pop, or burn out trying.

What further complicates the issue is the question of how hard is "hard?" It's a relative term. The strategies used by a 5.14 climber on a 5.14 route will be slightly different than those used by a 5.9 climber trying to bag a strenuous 5.9 route. The 5.9 route will require far less explosive strength and will most likely be more of an endurance test than a mat-ter of executing impossibly hard moves. With these mid-range routes, pacing and propitious resting are fundamental to suc-cess. On world-class testpieces, it's technique, experience, and explosive strength all the way. If you were to take the very crux off a world-class route and paste it onto a boulder, many climbers would be able to do it. The fact that a grim crux is preceded and followed by dire terrain is many times what makes the big-name routes so formidable. Here, it's a matter of the climber having an abundance of explosive strength, built up through years of climbing and training, and the shrewd conservation of that strength through good pacing.

Working a Route

Once the route approaches your technical limit, your chances of being able to climb it on your first try decrease. On a rugged, overhanging route there are so many decisions to make that your odds of making all the right ones the first time are remote. That's why it's news when somebody flashes a heralded testpiece. Ordinarily, trial and error is used to work these climbs out. As you keep repeating the first section, moving progressively upward, you'll find the best strategy for each section— how best to execute the moves, when to rest, and when to go like hell. That first bit will get easier because of your familiarity with it, requiring less work and leaving you with more reserves for the challenges ahead.

The value of having to siege a climb is that you quickly get an education on how to go about your work. You learn what works best for you, what your strengths and limitations are, and how to work with them. The point is, regardless of your level, it is worth your time to try to work out a difficult climb. Provided the route is not dangerous, go ahead and spend an afternoon falling off it. You'll probably learn more that afternoon than you would in a year of cruising routes well within your limits. The tricks of working a route will be taken up in greater detail later on.

NEW ROUTES

To establish a new route is to make a timeless statement. While many climbers like the timeless part—knowing their name will live on in guidebooks—an equal number forget the statement bit. Making a bad statement, thus a bad route, is to invite eternal infamy. So it's essential to do things right the first-time around, particularly if bolts are to be placed. I won't encourage or instruct climbers to establish new routes. Better to recall an incident that happened some years ago in the cafeteria at Yosemite.

I was with a Canadian climber who was then recognized as a master wall climber. Only 24, he'd already put up several new routes on El Capitan. A younger climber came to our table and asked my friend for advice about bagging big new walls. My friend suggested that our visitor go to some scrappy area where nobody ever climbed and experiment on short routes first. After he felt comfortable on one-pitch routes, perhaps then the young man could move on to bigger routes. Our guest, who already had a catalog of big walls to his credit, scorned this advice. After all, he noted, the first new climb my friend ever bagged was a Grade VI whopper on El

Capitan. "True," my friend stated, "but I didn't have to ask anyone how to do it."

Take a lesson from this. Make damn certain you know what you're doing before you start drilling, or you'll live to regret it. While nobody really can tell you how to go about establishing new routes, I can tell you a few things about how not to do it.

First, every sport has something—some procedure, some tangible entity—that is sacred. In boxing, you don't head-butt or hit low. In baseball, you don't touch the ump. In climbing, you don't doctor the rock. Ever. The rock does not belong to you, or even to your generation. Clearing off loose rock and detritus is one thing, but the second you start fashioning the stone for the sake of climbing, you're crossing the line and deserve whatever scorn is thrown your way.

Whenever you have to bolt, always remember that you have to hang your name on whatever you do. If you think the sheer technical difficulty of the route justifies modifying the rock, think about ten years ahead. Your blockbuster will be yesterday's news. But if it features fine positioning, stimulating climbing, novelty and class, it will be today's classic.

Lastly, always respect local ethics, and never alter an established route. Enough said.

Tips for Traveling: Different Media

Every climbing area is different. The more modes of climbing you familiarize yourself with, the richer your experience. If you lack funds or time to travel and experience different crags, try and remain open minded, and go easy on yourself if, when you do visit a new area and struggle to pick up relevant styles and techniques. Even experts don't master a new area straight out of the car. In time, yes. Only experience enables us to figure out the style and enjoy the success we all crave. Each time you learn something new, translate it back to your home turf.

The preparation for visiting a new area is to find out what type of climbing is involved, and practice that type. If you're going to a place where the holds are positive but far apart, hone up your big reach and dynamic skills; if you're heading towards pocketville, practice pulling on and stepping in pockets (but not too hard - you don't want to strain yourself before you get there); and if you're going somewhere super technical, get your techno skills up to speed. If you're going on a bouldering vacation, don't worry about endurance, but bring your overall fitness up so you can boulder until the cows come home. And if you're going to Yosemite, work at endurance and crack climbing skills, and prepare for some spectacular views.

CHAPTER 6

Bouldering and Freesoloing

Bouldering remains a favorite activity for climbers of all abilities. In a matter of an hour or two, bouldering allows you to climb tons, learn and practice new techniques, build strength and have a brilliant time climbing without gear. Hard bouldering is the best practice for cranking difficult cruxes. You always can do harder moves on boulders than you can on a rope, because you can try them ad nauseam. Moreover, if you do enough hard boulder problems, you will have executed, in one fashion or another, most every conceivable sequence. This helps you recognize similar sequences when you're out on the sharp end. From your mental logbook you can call up moves that worked before, and probably will work again. And whatever you run up against, it's most likely going to be easier, probably far easier, than what you have already cranked on the boulders.

In many ways, indoor climbing gyms, and in some cases, sport climbing areas, have come to replace bouldering as practiced by climbers in the past. Traditionally speaking, both gym climbing and clip and go routes are a form of roped bouldering; however both involve gear. The joy of bouldering is that it's just you and the rock—no standing around belaying, no clipping—nothing but chalking up and gunning it. However, extreme vigilance must be paid toward body control, since every time you fall, you hit the ground.

Spotting

Spotting is critical, and will make the difference between going for it or not. Spotting is much like belaying— you can save someone's life, neck, back, arm, wrist. And conversely, you can be saved. Learn all you can about good spotting— how best to cushion falls, to keep a climber's head off the ground, how to cushion a fall by placing your hands on a climber's back as they drop, and all the rest (covered shortly). Spotting is an art in itself, and some folks have even gained fame and notoriety from being prestigious, life - saving spotters. Get on that list!

For another point of view, let's listen to Nancy Prichard, former editor of *Rock & Ice* and a fine boulderer, break down some of the particulars:

"Bouldering is the simplest and purest of climbing pleasures, and is a proven way to perfect technique while giving a peerless all-around workout. Individuality is fostered, tenacity rewarded and, more often than not, both humor and humility are nurtured if not required. You need only shoes, a chalk bag and a rock—no gear, no partner. There are those few who blur the margin between bouldering and soloing—say, on high boulders—but as a general rule, traditional bouldering falls are not so severe as to kill or seriously hurt you. Downclimbing, acrobatic jumping, and various forms of spotting can lessen any risks. Ultimately, it's as dangerous as you make it. A good session yields a steady flow of adrenaline, which is welcome on dicey high moves and definitely addictive. Best of all, bouldering is a game of immediate gratification—summiting dozens of rocks in a single session. However if you're off-form, you may cry a river for never getting a body length off the deck. Recognized boulder problems tend to be hard, lest they'd be overlooked.

"Practice downclimbing and reversing moves. Lowering off dynos, reversing mantels, and wondering where the heck that balancey smear went helps save ankles while developing strength and technique. On longer problems, climbing up, then climbing down helps in working out the sequence. You wire the initial moves, ever going higher before reversing, familiarizing yourself with the sequence. When you are confident of your reservoir of strength and ability, you go for it. However, you can rarely reverse moves on boulder problems near or at your technical limit. It's task enough just to go up.

"Most good boulderers not only are good downclimbers, but great jumpers. If you boulder alone and don't flash every problem (and you won't), you'll eventually pump a hand out, a foot will blow off an edge, or some bungled move or another will cast you off. If you know where you are in relation to both the rock and the ground, you have an elevated chance of landing squarely on both feet. The spinning jump to the best landing spot, and the tuck-and-roll both work for emergency exits.

"Spotting is crucial when a boulderer is cranking upside-down (or is locked into any funky, awkward attitude), or the landing is poor. But even then some climbers refuse a spot, or favor only a "girl" spot. ("Grab me by my hips and gently lower me down.") Fine if you're Mr. Olympia spotting an anoretic sportclimber; but if you're a corn-fed dude and your girlfriend weighs 98 pounds, the spot is a sketchy one. The realistic goal of a spot is not to catch the climber, but to simply break the fall and keep the head from smacking solid objects. A shrewd spotter stands facing the rock in a volleyball setter position. When you are working out a hard bouldering problem, you might even hand-check with your spot, your hands gently on the climber's back or rump, ready to ease the inevitable the second it occurs. Two—even three—people spotting is not unheard-of if the situation demands.

"A great deal of bouldering is contemplative. Each problem is its own project. You complete one, then start afresh at the base of the next. If you fail, you have as many chances as you choose to try again. You try, fail, then sit, pondering your errors. While your forearms revitalize, you evaluate the

sequence, search for obscure edges and holds, and focus your efforts to match the physics of the problem. Then it's back at it.

"About bouldering technique: Practice, practice, practice. Bouldering requires different combinations of strength, contemplation and technique for different problems. Sequences often are not obvious; the more you boulder, the better you get at deciphering the correct sequence. Consider your body position relative to the rock, don't hold on too tight, and watch your footwork. The boulders are the best place to work on your lockoffs and mantels. Traversing offers a lot of mileage and short falls. And remember, if you're going to climb a certain rock, make certain you have an idea about how to get down. More than one ace has found herself marooned atop a high boulder, with the only immediate option being to try and reverse the hardest piece of climbing she's ever done. Poor sap.

"Limited commitment, little risk, adrenaline, satisfaction of getting to the top numerous times a day—bouldering is pretty much pure joy. It makes you strong, brave (should you go for the high ones), hones technique, and gives you good lies for social occasions."

Duane Raleigh, editor for *Climbing* and a leading climber in his own right, adds:

"Sheer simplicity is the true lure of bouldering: armed with a bag of chalk and a pair of comfortable rock shoes you can

A good brush and a well-placed sketch pad can come in mighty handy.

John Sherman photo

enjoy hours of sinew-ripping fun without the bother of ropes or even a partner. Yet, having a few inexpensive tools can increase your chances of success, and keep you from getting hurt.

"Every fall in bouldering is a grounder. Those three-to six-foot drops may seem insignificant, but those teeth-cracking jolts compound on each other and can eventually break you down, doing permanent damage to your ankles, knees, spine, and neck. Which is why no serious boulderer dares show his mug without a respectable "sketch" pad.

"A good sketch pad doesn't have to be much or expensive. The easiest one is simply your old ensolite pad, but you can do better than that. First, cut that ensolite in two. Next, get a hefty chunk of four-inch open-cell foam and sandwich it in between the two ensolite pieces. Use carpet glue to hold the thing together. Finally, get some closed-loop carpet and glue this to both sides of the ensolite. If you don't have the time or aren't in the mood to make your own pad, Kinnaloa and Black Diamond both make commercial pads, either of which works fine.

"Now that you have a burly pad that will take the sting out of most drops, all you have to do is make sure you land on it. It's tempting to place the pad directly under the first moves. But unless the crux is directly above the opening moves, setting the pad there is a mistake. Instead, scope the problem, boulder up to the crux and downclimb to figure out your fall trajectory. If the crux move is a straight-up-and-down one, place the pad directly underneath that section, but if the move is a lunge or diagonal slap, place the pad off to the side to account for your lateral swing.

"Okay, you have your pad, but you're still short a couple items. A small swatch of carpet, for instance, comes in handy for setting at the start of the problem. With the carpet thus positioned, you mount the rock with clean shoes.

"Another indispensable tool is the brush, or brushes because you actually need three. You'll use a toothbrush the most—for scouring off caked chalk and other hold scum that can hinder your grip. When a regular toothbrush doesn't cut it you need a beefier grout brush, like the type you find at the grocery store next to the 'Ajax'. When even a grout brush is too flimsy, go with a welder's wire brush, but use this tool sparingly—working a hold over with the wire can be self-defeating, as the abrasive bristles can make the holds slicker, especially if you're dealing with soft sandstone or limestone. For that reason, respectable boulderers only use a wire brush to knock off lichen and loose grit from their "projects" that haven't yet been climbed.

"Most of the time you can stand on the ground to brush the holds, but when that key grip is out of reach you need a "bubba" cheater stick, to which you can tape or otherwise lash a brush to and extend your reach. Almost any stick will do the job, but a six-foot rod of conduit has just the right stiffness and only costs a buck or so. While you're in the hardware store also pick up a couple feet of plastic tubing. A couple puffs through the tube will blast away any chalk or dust residue your brushes can't get; this is particularly useful for cleaning out pockets.

"Brushing and blowing off the holds before you get on a problem makes sense, but once you're done and ready to move on, give the holds a final hit with the tools. Doing so is just good manners, tantamount to toweling down the weight machines at Gold's gym.

"Try the really heinous problems only when you're fresh, and even then quit while you're still seeing success on most of the moves. Getting on a hard problem when you're tired or working it to the flailing point is bad for two reasons: It hurts morale, and worse, sets you up for future failure as your mind subconsciously remembers the things you do the most, making you prone to repeat them that way. Once you start seeing negative progress on a problem, move on to easier ground."

"But just how hard is that problem you've been trying? Pinning ratings to boulder problems is onerous at best. The conventional Yosemite Decimal System, which takes route length into account, doesn't quite work, as boulder problems tend to be but a handful of savage moves. Similarly, the "B" system, developed in the 1960s by legendary boulderer John Gill, is too vague as it compresses every problem between 5.11 and beyond into a paltry three grades: B1, B2, and B3. To clear up matters, John Sherman, has come up with his open-ended "V" scale, which is fast-gaining popularity. This system starts at V1 (somewhere around 5.10d) and currently goes up to V14, which seems to roughly correlate with hard 5.14+."

Virtually everyone contributing to this book has stated that bouldering is a prerequisite to arduous climbing. Specialists, who prefer the boulders to the crags, have pushed their art to mind-boggling levels of difficulty—far beyond what is found on the hardest clip-and-go routes.

Good rules to follow are:
• Never climb any higher than where you feel comfortable jumping from;
• If you must assume an upside down or awkward position, get a spot;
• Remember, if you fall off, you hit the ground. Always clear the ground of problem stones or any detritus that could cause twisted or broken ankles—the most common bouldering injuries;
• Lastly, strive to develop the boulderer's mentality: Any worthwhile problem takes dozens of tries. Try the impossible. And keep trying. Some day you just might make it. That's what bouldering is all about.

Craig Dillon photo

If a climber wants to risk his life, that's his decision, but to encourage anyone to solo is to reserve a place in hell. Consequently, talking about free soloing makes me a little edgy. It also makes my palms sweat. I've soloed just enough to know both the beauty and the horrors of the venture, and am leery of over- or understating either side.

Scrambling unroped over easy terrain is a required part of climbing. "Third classing" routes approaching your technical limit is not. Yet climbers do solo, and will continue to solo. So to ignore the topic altogether, to withhold information that possibly could save a person's life, seems recklessly mean and narrow-minded. Instead, I will pass on all that I can, hoping to limit the genuine risks.

No one argues that soloing is climbing in its purest form. That so few soloists fall suggests that sober, calculated judgement prevails over the naive notion of the foolish daredevil going off half-cocked. Herman Buhl, Reinhold Messner, Royal Robbins, and more recently, John Bachar and Peter Croft—some of the true legends of our sport—all have reputations fashioned, in part, from soloing. Still, while we laud these climbers, a definite taboo shrouds their exploits. Certainly, difficult soloing is reserved for the full-blown expert, for those who eat, sleep, and drink climbing. But even for accomplished soloists the practice is a minefield full of clear and subtle dangers. The likelihood is much overstated, but one should never get lured into soloing through peer pressure or dubious ambitions, like achieving fame. It's undeniable that many active climbers routinely solo easy, or even moderate, routes. A few solo desperate routes (5.11 and up). But I've also known plenty of world-class climbers who never solo, no matter how easy the terrain—and if anything, their reputations have grown from their forbearance. The point is, soloing is one aspect of the sport where you cannot, or should not, emulate other climbers.

What then, is the lure? By dint of the frank jeopardy involved, soloing evokes feelings of mastery and command, plus a raw intensity that even a million-dollar-a-year ball player will never experience: not in the Super Bowl; not in the World Series; not on center court at Wimbledon. And therein lies the snare. Following a particularly rewarding solo, when everything has clicked, the climber feels like a magician. These feelings can actually foster a sham sense of invincibility. Hence, it's not unheard-of that a narrow escape is followed by an eagerness to push things just a tiny bit further, and so on, until the soloist is courting doom. And he'll most assuredly find it if he doesn't quickly back off. The whole insidious business is closely tied to anything that is exhilarating, deadly, and fiendishly addictive. Whenever desire overrides judgement, bad things happen. If the soloing fool is fortunate, he'll have a harrowing close call, and he won't be the first to swear, "Never again!"

(opposite)

Peter croft solos the "Bearded Cabbage," Joshua Tree, California.

Bob Gaines photo

On the other hand, soloing has provided me with some of the sharpest, and greatest, experiences of my climbing career. Particularly on longer routes, the charged mix of fear and focus strips away any masks, exposing the most fundamental self. It's one way of finding out, once and for all, who you really are. It's also a sure way to die if so much as a single toehold pops. Understand this: The potential penalties simply are too high to rationalize risking your life to scale a section of stone. Wrap your reasoning in rarefied language, and maybe you'll touch on a vague truth. It's also true that my friend Tobin Sorrenson—a talented, beautiful, and outrageous young man—died while soloing the North Face of Mount Alberta. His death, at age 24, showed me the unforgiving side of the game, minus all the poetry and shimmering sunsets. It was a personal revelation of another, perhaps more significant kind. You just want to slog home and hug your child, kiss your wife, call your mom—tell someone you care about how much you love them. So when you're at the base, gazing up at the rock, review the soloist's code: "If there is any doubt about it, forget it!" If you do cast off, make certain you're doing so for your own good reasons.

CHAPTER 7

Indoor Climbing

Indoor climbing is the fastest growing segment of the climbing world. With its (normally) urban location and easy access, controlled environment and relative safety, the growth potential for gym climbing is virtually unlimited. (For a more in-depth look at climbing on artificial walls, check our other manual, *Gym Climb!*) Indoor climbing has become a popular and effective means of cross-training for all forms of climbing. Artificial climbing walls distill the basic concepts of climbing—grabbing holds, pulling, and then stepping on them—to their purest form. On a man-made wall your concerns are few. Without the distractions of weather, loose holds, suspect protection, route finding, or barking dogs you are free to focus all your energies on the moves.

Orientation

Understand that indoor climbing has nothing to do with climbing high peaks or weathering storms on El Cap. Indoor climbing never features dicey runouts on bad gear. In fact, much about gym climbing does not translate to the most benign roadside crag. Gym climbing has to a great extent become an end in itself. No question the experienced hand can buff technique and build strength in the climbing gym; but pumping plastic can never substitute for experience on actual rock. All of this, plus the popularity of climbing gyms, has given many of today's hotshots and weekend warriors a totally different orientation per actual rock climbing.

Particularly in bad weather areas, many climbers eschew the crags during winter months and stick to the gym. With its controlled climate, small fear factor (not counting fear of success and failure, which are very real fears), and easy access, many find they get more efficient training/climbing indoors than in standing around in the rain at their local crag.

Gyms offer mostly top roping and bouldering; certain select gyms offer very conservative lead climbing. Quickdraws are provided and spaced every body length (or less); belay devices are often bolted in the ground. A number of other responsibilities—that rest solely on you when you're at the crags—are provided entirely by the gyms. Remember that it's a whole different game out there on the rocks, where nothing can be taken for granted.

Caution

Gyms have brought climbing to the general populous, but the downside cannot be overlooked. Whenever you go outdoors, take great care and precautions. Read. Read. Read. Learn.

Learn. Learn. Take nothing for granted. Ever.

From Kansas City—where there isn't a hill in sight—to the swamp lands of Florida, climbers are learning ropes in the gym. The downside is that these climbers are denied first-hand experiences about the inherent risks of climbing outdoors. Accidents occur every weekend by the insurgence of inexperienced climbers hitting the crags with a gym mentality. Another risk factor is that today's sport climbers are pushing past limits rapidly, physical limits that is, because the risks are so reduced when you're climbing indoors. Of course it is possible to get hurt while climbing indoors, but generally the risks are far less compared to climbing outdoors.

Plus

The most common plus for plastic climbing is availability. You can climb in the evening as a working stiff. Even doctors like burl master Steve Hong can climb at an elite level because he's been able to take advantage of his home wall and the local gyms. A gym climber can presently crank from Topeka to Winnipeg to New York City. Young kids are now on the scene as well as moms and granddads. It's accessible to everyone.

On artificial walls you can exercise your creativity, as well as your body, by creating the routes of your dreams or nightmares, depending on your goals. You have the option of changing holds around, the very meaning of modular holds. You can do some of your most athletic climbing in an 8-foot-tall gym with 1000 square feet of climbing. You can extract your weakness by building or climbing indoor routes that exploit every flaw you have. Because indoor climbing route setters are getting more experienced, and the folks making artificial grips are using more detail, indoor climbing has become more intricate and subtle. With each passing year indoor climbing will more accurately replicate what is found outdoors.

But never exactly.

The Scene

Climbing gyms vary remarkably, but there are several constants. Most have short (25'- to 40'- high) walls with wartish, modular knobs. As mentioned, the early modular grips were rather crude. Current molds turn out a mind-boggling variety of holds—everything from huge, rounded bollards to one-finger pockets. The more sophisticated walls have inset pockets for variety, and feature sweeping angles, generally from overhanging to more overhanging. Either way, the climbing is usually basic pulling and hooking for the feet. In the almost complete absence of no-hand rests, indoor climbing tends to be more physical than on real rock.

Gripping and standing on plastic holds is no different from what you've already learned, but because most modular holds are either knobs, edges, or pockets it's essential to have a working knowledge of the pinky wrap (master this grip as it is usu-

ally the key to copping a quick rest), crimp, and pocket grips.

You grab plastic holds as if they were real rock, but the way you move on an artificial wall is noticeably different because of the simplicity and flat surface of indoor walls.

Kelly Jackson pulling on plastic at the Magic Mountain, Bellingham, Washington.

Cliff Leight photo

THE WALL

The European competition circuit has been promoted on a much grander scale than its American counterpart, so Europeans have more francs and Deutsche marks to spend on custom-designed walls, some of which are not far from art in their structure and relief. In America, where climbing industry money is in shorter supply, competitions have been staged on all manner of structures, including the side of luxury hotels and backpacking shops. Some recent competitions have opted for a less-permanent medium—namely, custom climbing panels lashed to construction scaffolds, with the ass-end of the whole rig anchored by a massive counter-weight to keep the wall static. These panels vary in size, but usually are about four feet square. They feature every conceivable type of hold—rounded nothings, underclings, side-pulls, comely jugs—the works. They also are machined to accept bolt-on holds, allowing each panel to be retro-fitted to whatever degree of difficulty the course setter desires.

A bigger series of panels has generally come to replace the old ones. In particular, EntrePrises has one-piece "molded" panels so authentic in their rock-like relief that some climbers prefer them to the real thing. The holds are not bolted on but part of the mold; and some of these panels are bigger than four meters square. Economics and practical concerns most likely will relegate the use of these super panels to climbing gyms and big-time regional and international meets.

Climbing difficulty is altered by changing the angle of the panel or by keeping the modular holds to a minimum; unlike the traditional bolt-on units, these panels often offer more climbing options—move for move—than an actual cliff.

Another popular design—featured in the superb "Rockreation" gyms—is a rock-hard plastic surface literally trowled or hosed onto a superstructure. The angle and relief of the wall is provided by a permanent superstructure, and the plastic provides the "skin" of the wall. Such walls are machine-gunned with countersunk bolts that accept modular holds. While the relief of the wall is unchanging, gyms frequently replace the holds, creating an endless succession of "routes" up the same terrain. As more and more gyms pop up, more competitions are being held in these hermetically controlled gyms.

A Typical Wall

There is no such thing as a typical wall. Every wall, like every climb, varies according to the designer and the available materials. However, there are several elements you are bound to see.

Organizers and wall designers love the overhanging stuff, so even novice routes often approach 90°. The angle depends on the scaffolding/superstructure configuration. As mentioned, rather than constructing a permanent wall or tooling out the wall of an existing building, some competitions are staged on temporary rigs composed of panels bolted to scaffolding. As each of the panels are hinged together, the climb tends to bulge in steps—for example, a vertical panel is followed by a 20° overhang, followed by another vertical one, and so on. The super-"molded" panels notwithstanding, each panel is relatively small. The contestant is continually reaching and yarding his feet over a bulge, and this often makes for awkward and jerky sequences. You never can get established on a four-foot piece of "rock," so only a very diminutive chap

A typical homemade wall.
Beth Wald photo

would feel at home on such a route. Nevertheless, that's what you're looking at in some cases.

If the competition does not utilize panels, you're dealing with some kind of edifice with bolted-on holds—most likely, the inside of a gym. Such routes make for more fluid climbing, owing to more fluid angles.

Home Walls

Home walls can be constructed with basic carpentry skills, though some home gyms are the product of very ingenious woodsmiths. The best solution to building your own home wall is to read books on the subject. Educate yourself and research what you need to make a bomber, fun wall. If you don't have carpentry skills, contact your local woodworker and see what it would take. It's relatively simple, based on basic building techniques. Three-quarter-inch plywood is a good base, though you must make certain to anchor the panels to very secure framing. Take extreme precautions in building your walls; they can make or break you.

Holds

Modular holds are made from various concoctions— ceramic, slippery resin, grit and epoxy, even wood. You can even bolt on rock fragments from the crags. Variety is a major plus to maximizing your fun. Holds, like route setting, are key to entertainment on artificial walls; with the right mixture you can play until your fingers are hosed, and never get bored.

When first introduced, one could talk in specific terms about the bolt-on holds. These days, they come in such variety that it's impossible to describe a "normal" bolt-on hold. The bulk of them are made using some type of resin base mixed with grit.

Competitions

There are many types of events in competitions, from elite "difficulty" meets, to "fun run" contests, speed climbing to bouldering, plus various gag/entertainment games, such as blindfold top-roping. Each class and type of event serves a purpose, and in some way benefits the other events. Serious regional, national, and international events generally are reserved for experts. But, as interest grows, more elite events are featuring all-comers competition as well as the headline meet. The reasons are simple. Climbers are, for the most part, action-oriented. Sure, it's entertaining to watch Rocket Cullpepper glide up the 5.14 route like it's a staircase; but if you've driven all the way from Amarillo, you'll want to sink your teeth into something more than the Cliff Bars that swarthy fellow is hawking on the sidelines. Climbers want, and will come to expect, some action of their own. In the future, look for many meets, regardless of size and prestige, to have an open category for the willing. After all, it's the entrance fees that supply many of the prizes.

Competitions do not establish who is the best climber. Many of the strongest, ablest climbers eschew competitions; they may fold at pressurized competitions; perhaps they're not interested in hanging around indoors for an entire weekend, waiting hours in a crowded isolation zone, with a dinky wall for 100 people to warm up on, and then having the honor of climbing a plastic route for 5 minutes. If you fall off, there goes your weekend. On even the most important meets, a competitor is lucky to climb more than a couple routes, barring the warm up zone. At the same time, training and preparing for competitions spark motivation and help you break through barriers. Some of your best climbing might come down in the training room.

Tactics

There are countless tactics to getting honed for competitions. Some people follow rigorous schedules, trying to time their peaking phases to the day of a competition. Others just wing it. Either way, it's only plastic, only a weekend gathered together with a bunch of other monkeys. So relax, have fun, explore yourself, your weaknesses and strengths through this medium. It can propel you to new levels, or it can send you to the depths if competing is not for you. Whatever the results, competitions should never lead a person to judge his being, his right to live a meaningful life, by virtue of success or failure on a string of modular holds.

Format

Competitions usually have a quarter-final open to anyone who registers. That round generally weeds out half the crowd for the semi-finals. The final is based on the top six to ten competitors for the men's and women's field. The finals are usually exciting and sometimes extremely tense.

Other competitions are like fun-run free-for-alls, where a stack of folk have a bunch of routes to try in a certain amount of time. You can choose the routes you want to climb, and you are scored on your top ten performances. These comps are generally more relaxed, and almost always more fun owing to the large participation.

Squabbling

Competitions are still wrought with problematic judging and inane squabbling over formats, rules, etc. But on the whole, competitions are a positive format to test yourself. As competitions become more popular, rules and procedures are becoming more uniform. It's a steep learning curve and there is much to be addressed. It should be a number of years until all of the bugs are out of the carpet, but in the meantime, competitions are valuable and most times a true riot. As media attention soars, competitions are being forced to provide some uniformity so the casual television viewer has a yardstick to understand what the hell is happening on the screen. Consider that fourteen-year-old Chris Sharma was picked up at the airport by ESPN on his way to winning a national competition. This sport is changing. As competitive climbing goes public, and is seen on TV, it's looking more and more like climbing has a shot at being an Olympic event. That's the wave of the future.

THE SET-UP

Again, no two competitions are alike. Some are now opting to toprope competitors, rather than rig the wall for the simulated lead. Perhaps it's more exciting to see your buddy pay for his mistake by plunging off the wall; but should a competitor catch his toe on the cord, spin upside down and smack his bean on the wall, we'll all be losers. So look for the toprope in all but the expert meets.

In most competitions you have an allotted amount of time—say 10 minutes—to complete each route. If the buzzer goes off while you're still climbing, your highest hold counts as your score.

The first competitions were loose, ill-defined affairs fraught with scandalous judging and national prejudices. The UIAA, a European-based climbing organization now has a Competitions Committee (CICE) that makes rules for and oversees international competitions. In the United States, the member organization of the CICE is the American Sport Climbers' Federation (ASCF), which in turn sanctions local, state, regional, and national competitions. In addition, the ASCF chooses a national team for representation at international events, and provides a training program for judges.

The ASCF focuses its efforts in two ways: sanctioning

competitions for organizers, and providing a numerical ranking for climbers. Competitors gain points at local and regional competitions that allow them ultimately to compete for a place on the national climbing team. Such point ranking also allows potential sponsors of climbers to see how good they really are.

Membership in the ASCF is available at several levels. An individual who wishes to compete and gain standing can join for $25. Anyone with an interest in organizing or competing can reach the ASCF at 35 Greenfield Drive, Moraga, CA 94556. (510) 376-1640. (www.climbnet.com/ascf).

Optimize

You'll have only a couple of minutes after coming out of isolation before getting on the wall. Make sure that you've warmed up. Stretch and get your fingers, arms, toes, and hands ready. Keep limber, relaxed, focused, and ready to crank!

Beth Rodden, 1996 Continental Championship, Vancouver, British Columbia.

Stewart M. Green photo

Eat wisely before competing. Many climbers go with quick-energy bars or carbo drinks shortly before their heat, getting the volts without the bulk. (Mind you, each competition has a handful of dead-serious competitors who look like they've just survived 50 days at sea in a life jacket. With .00002 percent body fat, their keen faces drawn and pinched, you hope they win so they can finally enjoy a square meal.)

Competition climbing is more of a mental game than sport-climbing at the crags. You have to block out all the crowd/announcer racket, concentrate, execute hard gymnastic moves, plus deal with the pressure of being "on the spot." If you blow a move and slip, you're out of there—you cannot lower and try again. Under these circumstances, it might be better to be a little nervous and really focused than to be utterly relaxed and calm.

Success

While few of us go to these events with even remote hopes of winning, let's be honest enough to admit that we'd rather make a good showing than a poor one. To that end, let's pick the minds of those who have competed at the big meets and see if we can't get a small edge over the rest of the competitors. First, let's listen to Hans Florine, national speed-climbing champion:

"Things to contemplate in isolation before competing: Remember, "the route goes." You must assume that the course setter designed the route so it will go, and you have to believe you're as good or better a climber than the course setter. Visualize clipping that last quickdraw or climbing the entire route and topping out.

"When warming up, do not get involved with other com-

Steve Hong on Men's Final Route, National Championship, San Francisco.

Stewart M. Green

petitors (especially those better than you) in a bouldering contest on the warm-up wall. The quickest way to get rid of competition is to have them dyno for some one-finger pocket. Don't laugh. This happens. Everyone takes a different amount of time to recover. Try to get your forearms fully pumped on the warm-up wall then have at least an hour's rest before getting on the competition wall. However, you should warm up your fingers just before getting on the competitive route.

"Things to remember while on the route: The sequences are more limited than on the crags. With that in mind, try to quickly pump through the moves, rather than hanging out to scope them. If you're at a genuine resting place, where you can momentarily de-pump, then snatch a quick look at the rest of the climb. But always be looking above, figuring out the next sequence. If the rest is marginal and you see a probable sequence above, go for it. You'll probably do better than if you hung out running sequences through your head, getting all the more tired before trying the moves. If the competition involves simulated leading, remember that the course setter wants you to make the clip, so count on a moderate rest, or a pause, at each quickdraw. If the clip feels awkward and strenuous, climb a little higher until it feels easier.

"Above all else, know the rules before you get on the route! Know how much time you have to complete the route. Know what is on and off the route. On some routes, panel edges may or may not be used."

Alison Osius is a senior editor of *Climbing*, a four-time member of the U.S. Climbing Team, and a proven performer on the international circuit. Her competitive experience is principally with elite meets, but her counsel is germane to any competition. Says Alison:

"All "plastic" climbing has much in common, so spend time on practice walls and learn what to expect. You're always learning and storing up tricks you can later use for a competition. Generally, the moves are more straightforward than on rock— holds stand out and the options are fewer. Learn the common moves, like the "flag," where a free leg passes behind the set leg and extends out behind you close to the rock as a counterbalance. This helps check the barn-door effect, while at the same time placing your weight more squarely over your set foot. There are limited holds, so be ready to place a foot on the same hold your hand still occupies, or has barely left. Always practice getting rests. One technique that's particularly useful when you're pumped is hooking your hand around a hold, so that you're weighting the section of hand between wrist and pinky. You can use your feet on rock edges to pull your weight close to the wall—even more so on plastic holds. And practice downclimbing, so that you can do it confidently when you hit a puzzling move during a competition. By reversing to your last rest, you can regain strength and psyche, and can take another look.

"When competing, make certain everything is as light as possible— no huge chalk bag, no Clydesdale harness, no figure-8s or locking crabs or widgets hanging off your back. Break in a new pair of shoes for competition by climbing in them for about three weeks. Set them aside before they get much more worn.

"The night before an event, pack all your gear— chalk bag, chalk bag string, shoes, jacket or sweatshirt, and outer pants if you want them. I pack a little bottle of rubbing alcohol and a toothbrush to clean my shoes just before I go out. Take an extra pair of socks to wear over your shoes as you walk out to the wall.

"Walkman? Check. Tapes? Check. It's great when they let you climb to your own music, but I've twice now gone to the pleasant trouble of picking out tunes, then—curses!—forgotten my John Denver cassette.

"Optional: Needle and thread and maybe a small pair of

scissors. They come in handy for all kinds of things. Also, a book or magazine or pen and paper—you could be waiting a good long time for your turn on the wall. Recently, Will Gadd of Canada drew to climb last—and waited 10 hours! Depending on the venue, you may or may not be served food while (if) you wait. I always bring a small water bottle and some food. (For me, that's a banana and a Power Bar). Go with what you usually do. You're best-off with fruit and complex carbs before the event.

"Even if you're staying in a hotel, consider bringing your own food for breakfast. Again, you don't want to deviate much from what you usually have. I bring cereal and some dried milk.

"Okay. You've eaten breakfast, arrived, and signed in. Backstage, in 'isolation,' everyone's languishing around. I quite like this part, lying around, talking. Every competition should have a practice wall or area, or at least some gym equipment. Most climbers prefer to get a good pump, maintain it for about ten minutes, then lose it about an hour prior to competing, but it's hard to manage that as you don't know exactly when you'll climb. All you can do is estimate, based on the time limit per competitor, and recalculating as contestants come and go. Also, beware of getting caught out in the cold. People sometimes are called onto the rug when they thought they still had an hour to wait.

"Each person's pre-climb ritual is as individual and personal (and embarrassing) as what we each do in front of the mirror. My custom is not very elaborate (that's pre-climb custom, not my mirror capers, which are none of your business), and deals mostly with audio-visuals. I remember great and inspired climbing performances I've seen, and certain comments I've heard. I hear Jim McCarthy saying, as he watched Scott Franklin smoothly pulling up on one hold after another at the first Snowbird World Cup, 'Scotty's climbing well,' or England's Martin Atkinson, at the World Cup in Leeds, England, saying as Robyn Ebersfield cruised up the wall, 'Got a cool head for competitions, doesn't she?' I remember a line from a *Life Magazine* story about the climbing world's top female dog, Lynn Hill. Referring to an upcoming event, she said, 'When I go out there, everything will be crystal clear.'

"Well—time to go out. Not to tempt fate, but, if anything unseemly happens, like you trip or stumble or walk past the wall, put it straight out of your mind. You need to be humorous and no-nonsense with yourself, particularly on the wall. In Berkeley several years ago, I had an awful slip and was very lucky to catch myself on the fly. 'Don't even think about it,' I mock-scolded. Ten feet later, I did fall off, and only as I was lowering did I remember the slip.

"Overall, I think the biggest mistake inexperienced people make is not looking around enough. Plan, plan, plan—starting during the time period (usually two minutes) you're given to inspect the wall. Look at the moves absolutely as hard and far as you can, imagining probable sequences. Look around

corners and arêtes and above roofs and memorize where holds are. You may want to pick out a corresponding notch, rivet, or hold—something—on the near- or under-side of a feature, in case once you're underway you can't lean out to spot holds. I learned the hard way to look over the quickdraws all the way up the route. At Leeds, I got under a roof, leaned out and peered over the lip only to see no holds. I finally spotted a quickdraw about eight feet out right. By the time I saw it, I'd lost some strength. The point is, I hadn't traced the route's whole line via the quickdraws.

"On the ground, however, I was looking hard at the wall but couldn't see how to do the first crux, through the first little roof. The timer told me my time had started, but I thought, "I can't go, I don't see how to do this." I made myself stand still until suddenly, I saw the sequence. The move took down several people, but I was okay because I could go quickly and avoid getting pumped. The point came home again when I was watching Didier Raboutou on the superfinal. He spent long moments beyond his allotted viewing time mostly scrutinizing a funky low move. It was worth it.

"Be optimistic, and just concentrate on the moves. Don't think about where so-and-so might have gotten to, or what

Liv Sansoz, 1995 World Cup, Villach, Austria.

Dougald MacDonald photo

place you hope to get. Just get up there and do the job.

"As you begin, remember to breathe. Look for rests. And let yourself enjoy the climbing. The more you like the route and the holds, the better you'll do.

"When you need to be dynamic, think in terms of power glides rather than lunges. If you must lunge, commit to it all-out, and remember to grab.

"When you come to a hard part, don't be tempted to thrash on through. Hang on. Figure it out. But when you have to go for it, go fast. For example, if you reach a hold above a roof, swoop those feet right up.

"Look several moves ahead. You may not have time to tinker on a roof; holds can go from decent to time-bomb so fast. If you don't see from below that you have to get a hold with a certain hand, you may realize it too late.

"Forget the crowd, seductive as its presence and voices are. It can make you feel as if you're doing better than you are, and can goad you on too soon. At Leeds, Catherine Destivelle stepped up and down three times at one ugly little roof before making a try and popping off. Afterwards, she said she had let herself be swayed by the shouts of 'Allez!' and 'Go for it!' from below. 'I hear ze crowd and I am . . . entranced,' she said, chuckling. 'And so I go, even though I am not all right in my mind for ze move. In ze future, I must listen only to myself.'

"Okay, you've hit trouble, and your demise is nigh. Never just give up—when you think you can hang on no longer, you probably can eke out one more move—and never grab the rope (horrors!). 'At least die trying,' as John Long (rogue that he is) wrote in *The Only Blasphemy*. You might latch that hold after all. And then another, and another, and isn't that what it's all about?"

An exemplary treatise, granted. But Ms. Osius leaves one question unanswered: What does our darling do in front of her mirror?! She says just a little "air-climbing" (a climber's version of shadow-boxing), but she's too tall and too smart to be believed here.

The mighty Lynn Hill (five-foot zero, 101 lbs.) is one of the most famous rock climbers in the world. She deserves to be. On a competitive circuit clogged with Europeans, Lynn was many times over the world champion. Moreover, her adventure climbing exploits are no less distinguished—harrowing El Capitan peg-ups, first free ascents of wilderness walls, the first free ascent of the Nose, on El Cap for Pete's sakes. She's done it all and always with such power, grace, and style that even her staunchest rivals applaud her success. She is a true champion. Let's conclude our business here by listening to Lynn's views on competitions, knowing that her insights will serve us on all genres of climbing:

"Good or bad, competition is a quality inherent in human nature. It has been, and most likely will continue to be, a factor in human evolution.

"Competition was a driving force in climbing long before

the first organized meets took place. Climbers the world over always have strived to climb faster, higher, in better style, without bottled oxygen, etc. In so doing, climbers have competed against one other, against the rock or mountain, and always against themselves.

"Initially, organized competitions stirred a great controversy among many top European and American climbers. For various reasons, many of these climbers boycotted the first competition, held in Bardonecchia, Italy, in 1985. Once climbers understood that competitive climbing was a separate game that neither infringed or demeaned climbing on natural rock—and that there was money to be made—most hold-outs chose to compete in the second annual Sport Roccia competition, also held in Italy, in 1986. This was my first experience in a free-climbing competition.

"This 1986 competition showed how hard it was to organize and structure a fair and consistent venue to measure performance. It could hardly be otherwise for a new sport, and I was not surprised that the rules and format were vague and poorly thought out. I was completely shocked, however, when the meet organizers changed the rules to enable a well-known European climber to win!

"There were other disturbing aspects of this competition as well. The match was held on a cliff some ways off the road, and hundreds of spectators completely ravaged the verdant hillside getting there. From the base, the viewing was excellent—because all the trees had been chopped down! The rock was trashed as well; holds were chipped, pockets were plugged up with cement, all to create routes of the desired difficulty.

"Though they should have been the primary impetus, environmental considerations did not spur on the development of artificial walls specifically designed for competitions. Rather, bad weather, convenience of location (for spectators and the media), and the ease of fashioning fair and perfectly-tailored routes quickly made artificial walls the preferred medium for virtually all competitions.

"Despite the refinements in design, artificial walls are by no means a perfect simulation of natural rock, nor is climbing in a competition comparable to climbing with friends at a favorite crag. Competitions and artificial walls are simply another facet of climbing, one that provides a new form of play, fresh challenges, and a novel kind of learning experience. As a result of competing, I have learned much about myself with respect to the psychological elements of the game, while my actual climbing prowess has steadily improved.

"Since all actions are directed by the nervous system, either by conditioned responses or automatic reflexes, the brain is key in determining one's physiological potential. Genetics, natural ability, physical training, and experience, also are critical factors in reaching one's potential. Yet one's attitude is no less vital to success—that conscious element

Shelly Presson on women's final route, National Championships, San Francisco.

Stewart Green photo

that we are free to cultivate and improve through a better understanding of ourselves.

"There are many talented climbers capable of winning on a given day. Most have the necessary strength, technique, and experience to win. What generally prevents a person from optimum performance are mental distractions, or mental blocks. Through my own experiences, and observation of others in many competitions, I have identified a whole range of mental errors. High anxiety is the most common; it usually stems from a lack of confidence or a fear of failure. This most likely expresses itself when full concentration and confidence are needed most. A momentary mental distraction during a crux move has sent more than one anxious competitor off the wall. Anxiety simply wastes strength. You tense up, overgrip handholds, and climb stiffly and awkwardly. Your thinking becomes limited and rushed, and often you commit to a hastily-planned sequence. You also can create excess anxiety by placing too much importance on winning. This attitude inhibits your ability to relax and directs your thinking contrary to what you'll need to perform optimally. Generally, you'll perform best when you have a true desire to climb for the inherent pleasure it brings.

"We all have off days, when the desire and spark simply are not there. If an off day coincides with a competition, more effort is needed to redirect one's state of mind. In such cases, I try to reinforce positive performance qualities and review certain mental affirmations. I imagine how I would like to perform, rather than how I'd like to feel. Override negative thoughts and feelings by feeding yourself positive performance goals. Since my best climbing experiences occur when I have an intense desire to climb, I overcome ennui by recreating this state of mind. Before competing, I recall positive climbing experiences, remembering as vividly as I can how I felt on those special days, thereby reinforcing a similar level of concentration, sense of rhythm, and enthusiasm.

"During the warmup period, I concentrate on moving in a relaxed fashion, without exerting any more energy than necessary. Just before climbing, I close my eyes and enter a progressive relaxation ritual, scanning my body for any sensation of tension. If I find any tense spots, I focus on releasing that tension. I also cultivate a sense of well-being, while reaffirming my intention to climb focused and relaxed. In the isolation area, it's usually possible to hear clapping and shouting from the audience. This can greatly magnify one's level of excitement and anxiety, particularly if the person climbing before you is performing well. But after dozens of competitions, I've learned to deal with these pressures. Although competition measures the ability of each person relative to the others, it should not be considered a 'battle' between contestants, or even a fight against the wall. The people I compete 'against' are a community of friends and peers with whom I share my passion for climbing.

"Rather than charging the wall like a gladiator, I direct my thinking in a way that allows me to be clear and confident. I maintain a balance between my level of excitement and relaxation. Whether I am climbing at a competition or at a crag, I can shine only if I reach this state. Only then can I react intuitively, creating a sort of harmony between my actions and what the climb requires. As soon as it becomes a battle, I tense up, can no longer react naturally, and the harmony is lost.

"The trick is to realize the qualitative difference between 'fighting,' and focusing my efforts and desire to respond to the best of my ability.

"My actual competition strategy is simple: At the wall, I take enough time to look around, to perceive all possible holds and devise the probable sequence. Once I decide on a sequence, I commit 100% of my focus and effort to it, no matter how desperate it seems.

"On days when everything flows together, I reach a state of pure concentration that allows me to be keenly perceptive and to react spontaneously. These are the experiences I seek, whether I am in a competition or simply climbing for myself."

We could spend 50 pages examining the physical aspects of competition climbing and never exhaust the topic. On the other hand, Christian Griffith, a member of America's first climbing team, thinks an appropriate mental outlook is the most important factor. Says Christian:

"I have heard many competitors tell me about their 'positive attitude' before a big meet. Many of these climbers fall in the first 15 feet. Competitions are mentally taxing, so never mind the sham 'positive attitude,' which is most times a means to rationalize failure. A good competitive showing is a great experience, and a poor one is mortifying— don't waste time and energy thinking about either before the event. Enter the competition with a blank mind, and your body will perform to the best of its experience and training. It's this vacant, 'silent observer' state that has seen me through my best ascents. The degree to which I can attain this state determines my success in competitions."

Route Setting

There is a new federation called the ALF: American League of Forerunners. The ALF is composed of a group of climbers that have been certified to set routes for competitions, gyms, etc. Basically, ALF teaches climbers to set great routes. Route setting in your own home gym can bring tremendous satisfaction. Experiment with turning holds in unusual ways, concocting interesting, fun, challenging and beautiful moves. Route setting is a very creative outlet that allows you to share something wonderful with others. Your friends will thank you for good routes.

So far as the competitive circuit goes, there are many variables that affect how a course will be set. First, one must consider how easy and fast can the holds be changed? It ranges from the relatively easy—screwing holds into pre-existing holes—to breaking out the masonry drill for each hold—an epic and time-consuming task. Also, things can and do go wrong, even with painstaking planning—wrong tools, stripped bolts, inherent wall engineering snafus, a lack of time, it's 10 minutes until the competition begins, etc. Any or all of these problems make the course setter's job a tough one, and will affect the route he/she sets.

Designing a course often is as taxing as climbing it. Generally, course setters try and fashion a route that gets progressively more difficult without forcing everyone into a fall at the same place. Such a strategy means the setter must take into account factors like reach, men and women climbers, and the desires of sponsors and judges while trying to feature a panoply of moves including dynos, thin stuff, tricky bits, gorilla cranks, Frankenstein liebacks, etc. Usually, the course setter is faced with at least one ongoing nightmare—like when it's three o'clock in the morning and the power goes down. When this happens, the course setter usually is trashed from climbing 2,000 feet on the wall while working out the sequence. Many artificial walls aren't "meet ready" until sunrise, if that early. Time, or the lack of it, is a constant problem. Most competition walls require expensive rental equipment (scaffolding, lights, etc.), as well as space fees, so the essential "extra" days needed to properly set the course usually don't exist. For the most part, course setting is a thankless job. Though he can literally make or break a competition, a course setter's only solace is to either kick back and reap the praises of a gem route, or endure the tongue lashings of a bad one.

Most course setter's decisions are based on many of the factors mentioned above, as well as any special requests of the event promoter and sponsors. Most meet organizers want an exciting course for both spectators and climbers. Thus, a common course consists of a number of power moves topped by more dynamic moves as the "summit" nears. Seasoned steers take into account natural conditions. If the wall is in the sun and it's humid and greasy, experienced hands will skip the slopers and tweakers and go with more positive holds and ingenious sequences—like side pulls and underclings. It's always good to throw in a jumbo dyno somewhere as well, even if it's jug to jug. In cool, shady conditions, look for hard sequences, including a few dime cranks and some pumping slope jobs as well. If the wall is long—say, over 40 feet—it probably will involve more spread-out moves, as opposed to crunch work, which is used to maximize limited wall space. Overall, most courses get increasingly difficult and pumping as you go higher. Often, a tricky, but effective rest position is devised somewhere on the wall. When competing, be aware of this possibility. Any experienced course setter will factor in the weather and natural conditions, as well as strive after fun moves, install a really spectacular sequence somewhere, try to build in a requisite pump sequence, and not try to bust a climber's chops by requiring crimpy dime pulls at the crux. All of these things should help a competitor second-guess the decisions of the course setter. Also, if you know what kind of climbing the course setter favors, you're bound to see his pet techniques employed on the course.

If the competition entails simulated leading, expect to get

a semi-rest at some of the clips. No doubt there will be some hard clips as well, but not every clip will be a desperate one. This allows a competitor little step-by-step goals—keeping the confidence up—as opposed to the one big goal of reaching the top.

The competitors generally don't affect a setter's decisions in designing a route. Nor do they strive after a certain rating. Most concentrate on eliminating "X" number of people per round, ultimately terminating all but one—the winner.

Present-day walls are better engineered, allowing design of more spectacular routes for both climbers and spectators. Also, as more money is available, events are becoming better organized and less rushed, allowing more time to both set courses and compete. Expect categories will expand. Speed climbing will become more popular, and rehearsed difficulty—worked routes—will take the spotlight. Competitors will be younger (as in gymnastics competitions), but in at least some cases, experience will favor the older, stronger climbers (as in surfing contests). Presently, colleges and schools will have climbing teams, and local, regional, and national competitions are starting to come into their own.

RAW SPEED

I can't leave off competitions without reviewing what is quickly becoming the show-stopper of every venue that features it: speed climbing.

First seen in Eastern European countries (particularly in the Soviet Union), speed climbing has become an increasingly important part of most American competitions, depending on the size and timetable of the meet. Speed climbing events generate a lot of interest and rave reviews. From a spectator's point of view, speed climbing is far more exciting than the technical event.

The courses usually are set up to allow rapid passage, featuring long and wild dynamic climbing between jug holds. Get a mad-dog speed climber chomping at the bit, goaded on by a couple hundred pushy spectators and a joker on the mike, and watch out! The 100-yard dash has nothing over this event. At the recent Extreme Games, staged by ESPN sports and beamed all over the globe, the speed climbing championships (won by Hans Florine in back-to-back years) was hands down the highlight of the climbing coverage. Look for this event to grow in popularity.

For those interested in speed climbing, let's cue up Hans Florine, who routinely takes the gold at speed climbing events:

"I imagine I am throwing the holds to the ground. Generally, you can do two short moves faster than one long dyno, which saps strength for the following moves. Forget the methods of conventional 'difficulty' climbing, where you grab a hold, reposition your hand on it, milk it, huff off it, crimp on it, chalk off it, and finally crank off it. Almost all com-

petition speed routes are 'jug hauls,' so work the holds with that in mind. Usually, you're allowed to watch other competitors climb the route: take advantage of that opportunity and study their moves. I've filched at least two moves at every competition by watching other speed climbers at work and this has given me faster times on the wall. If you're allowed to rehearse the route prior to the competition, try to work out a good sequence for the last 10 to 15 feet, because that's where you are apt to be pumped and stupid. There usually is a bell or buzzer on the top of the wall, so never fail to hit it!"

John Cronin on Semifinal route, Tour de Pump, Colorado Springs.

Stewart M. Green photo

Jim Thornburg on "Rude Boys," Smith Rock, Oregon.

Kevin Powell photo

CHAPTER 9

Training

Climbing plastic routes is an end in itself, but the pros also treat artificial walls as training grounds for developing their strength, endurance, and on-sight abilities. Additionally, they use them to duplicate the real rock routes they intend to tick in the coming climbing season.

Strength training is as simple as getting on routes that are too hard for you to link in their entirety— those that you can climb by doing the moves bolt-to-bolt. Or, if you lack a partner, you can work on your strength by traversing the base of the wall or by climbing in the bouldering cave—a common area in climbing gyms.

The concept behind strength training on plastic is the same as strength training with weights— brief spurts of savage intensity, followed by long rests. To do this, crank off five to seven moves (the equivalent of a weight lifters "reps") that are right at your limit. Take a five-minute rest before continuing. Repeat the process five to seven times.

To build your endurance, pick routes, or better, long traversing boulder problems that are a couple grades below your max and climb until you pump off. As you climb, be careful to avoid rests and shakes—these are counterproductive to enduro training. After a couple minute's rest, get back on the wall and continue. Repeat until the gym closes.

Add-on

A fun game called "Add-on" is also great for building endurance and memorizing sequences. To play add-on you need a partner of similar ability and a spray of holds close to the ground. The game goes like this: get on the wall and crank off five (mostly traversing) moves. Drop off. Your partner gets on the wall, repeats your moves, then tacks on five of his own. Repeat this scenario until you're dusted, which for most people is somewhere around 30 moves; but can go beyond 100 moves for ultra conditioning—physically and mentally.

Study the route from the ground. Cracking the sequences when you're by the Coke machine is less strenuous than trying to solve them on lead. If you can't decipher a section, look at the finishing hold and then reverse down until you get to the trouble spot. Once you get your sequences figured out, jump on the route and stick to your plan. Commit to your sequence, but if you get into trouble, look around and come up with a new solution. If you find yourself crossed up, hang in there, figure it out as best and efficiently as possible, and carry on.

Pointer

A simple game called "Pointer" is excellent for honing your on-sight skills. As with add-on, this is mostly a traversing exercise and requires a partner. Get on the wall and climb, but only use the holds your partner is pointing to. If you're the person doing the pointing, time it so that you stay barely one step ahead of the person doing the moves. A good route setter keeps the climber struggling, but doesn't make it so hard he falls right away. A round of pointer ends with a fall, and then the pointer becomes the climber.

Other good exercises include climbing super-fast and really slow. Mixing up your pace this way adds interesting variety, but will also bring out your deficiencies, which can go unnoticed if you always climb the same way.

MONSTERS

Sport climbing champions are a testament to hard core training and dedication. Ruthless, rigorous hours of training, forcing one's body past barriers with skin at its rawest, while challenging the mental psyche with intense regiments, is creating climbing power houses—monsters, if you will. These new and very intense training regiments are taking sport climbing into the future. And the beauty is its accessibility. Most hard cores—and medium to light cores, for that matter—currently train indoors, either on their home walls, or at their local gyms.

It's no longer a frustrating game of waiting for the good weather. You can get grueling, fun workouts indoors—in a t-shirt and shorts—when outside it's snowing like the North Pole in January. In conclusion, let's look at specifics according to Dan Cauthorn. Dan has been the director of the Vertical Club in Seattle, Washington since 1987, and has more experience in designing workout programs (relative to climbing gyms) than anyone else in the United States. Dan offers the following suggestions:

Endurance

"General stamina is essential for climbing, but most important is localized endurance in the climbing-specific muscles. Endurance climbing at a rock gym means lots of climbing, especially on big holds. You don't want to crimp on small holds and let finger pain be the limiting factor. The all-out, deep tissue, forearms-feel-like-wood pump is the desired result of an endurance workout. Continuous, uninterrupted climbing is best. On a bouldering wall, a good beginning routine is to traverse back and forth. Think of Spiderman as you shuffle across the wall. Try not to get too crossed up reaching over yourself. Instead, strive for smooth movement. Shift your weight carefully, rest between strenuous moves and keep track of your time. Thirty minutes of continuous climbing is an attainable goal. Another endurance training technique is intervals up and down a toprope wall. Pick a difficulty level well within your limit. Maintain good technique; it will only make the laps easier. Be creative linking walls and routes.

"Remember, if you just can't get pumped on a vertical wall, don't move onto smaller holds. Get onto a steeper wall where the holds are larger still but the pull of gravity is that much more severe. Cave climbing is the epitome of steep climbing on big holds.

Strength

"Every climber wants to be stronger. Strength feels good, and it allows you to climb harder routes. The strength workout at the rock gym is bouldering or red points (including toprope red points). Crank away on hard problems with good rests between burns. Again: warm-up, don't forget to breathe, and strive to stay relaxed—even when cranking through cruxes. Use the rating system to keep track of your progress. Breaking through the threshold into each higher rating is one of the more rewarding moments for every climber. The 5.10 level is traditionally a major step for recreational climbers. Rely on good fundamental technique and prior endurance training to pique your ambition.

Doug Englekirk at the 1992 Snowbird Competition.

Kevin Powell photo

"Even though bouldering is an extreme workout, it is still primarily a problem-solving task. Reading skills—that is, quickly figuring out the sequence to a crux—are for some climbers intuitive and for some, analytical. In any event, difficult climbing is physically taxing. It takes discipline not to overdo it.

Strategy

"Besides a daily idea of what you will do in the gym (warm-up, endurance laps, etc.), formulate weekly and seasonal tactics. A varied gym routine alternating with cross training and rest days is the best way to use a rock gym. Without a strategy, you're much more likely to get injured, burned-out, or both.

"Let your gym use evolve with the seasons. For example, winter months are a time to build a base of endurance; early spring workouts might emphasize strength with more bouldering sessions. During the summer, maintain technique and finger strength between weekend climbing. Take the month of December off entirely to shop and party."

PEAKED

Recognize the difference between being in good overall shape, and being absolutely peaked. Good fitness actually makes you less injury prone. But when you're peaked, you're working at the extreme edge of your physical capabilities and it becomes increasingly possible to overextend yourself; if anything, your body is so highly tuned that it is fragile, in a sense. There are loads of scientific explanations as to why the highly-tuned race car will break down faster than the family wagon. It's also known that if you run a race car at top speed for too long, it eventually will blow up. The problem was best described by Whitey Herzog, ex-manager of the St. Louis Cardinals. He was amazed with the conditioning and prowess of modern ball players. He likewise was concerned with how fragile they were, a problem he ascribed to absurdly strict dieting. The players simply were too highly tuned to last the duration of a 162-game season. Whitey suggested that once a week his players go out and eat a rare steak and a slab of pie to "get a little juice on the bone." They did. Injuries tapered off to minor sprains and the Cardinals won the World Series.

So whatever nutritional program you choose, it should correspond to the cycles of your training and climbing. If your climbing has no cycles, no breaks, if you continually try and stay at your maximum (and whippet-thin), you're going against virtually every modern sports philosophy.

GENERIC TRAINING/CROSS TRAINING

Weights

Weight training is an effective way to improve overall body conditioning. The main advantages of a good weight training routine are that you can significantly increase both strength and endurance with no increase in body weight, providing you watch your diet. High strength-to-weight ratio is the aim. A good workout with weights also helps mitigate the fatigue and lack of power that is the bane of most climbers. Climbers who already have technical ability, but lack that last bit of hoist, are best served by such a routine. Others are advised to spend time on the rocks until technique is polished. Once that's accomplished, a cross-training routine is bound to improve performance. Understand that the best strength program cannot make you a heroic climber. At best, strength only can help amplify existing talents.

Any routine you borrow or develop yourself should incorporate certain physiological laws and techniques that often are ignored by climbers, though they are followed religiously by serious weight lifters. The first law is: Train the whole physique, not just the muscles associated with climbing movements. Ignoring muscles with an opposite but complimentary function (antagonistic muscles) produces an imbalanced machine, and makes one injury prone for a number of reasons. It's fine to emphasize

Suggested weekly training strategies:

Off-Season

Monday—technique/endurance

Tuesday—rest

Wednesday—strength

Thursday—rest

Friday—technique/endurance

Saturday—cross train or strength

Sunday—cross train

On-Season

Monday—rest

Tuesday—strength

Wednesday—cross train

Thursday—technique/endurance

Friday—rest

Saturday and Sunday—climb

sport-specific muscles, but not at the exclusion of the rest of your body. The second law is: Pick a muscle group, do exercises that best isolate those muscles, and trash them. The third law is: Allow muscles 48 hours to recover before blasting them again.

Ignore any of these precepts and you'll get something less than maximum results. Know that these precepts are not based on any training philosophy or opinion, but rather are based on physiological laws. No one made of flesh-and-blood can get around them.

There are hundreds of books from which a novice climber can draw from to develop a general weight-conditioning program. Whichever one you decide upon, the best results will come by focusing on the most fundamental movements, which best blast the muscles. Always adhere to a policy of strict form. Try to execute the exercises perfectly. This adherence to form will carry over to your climbing. Form always is more important than the amount of weight you are trying to heft. Your focus should be placed on general muscular conditioning, improving technique, and staying uninjured.

As your ability takes you into the mid-level grades (5.9 or 5.10), you'll want to decrease your gym training (iron work) and begin some of the more specific climbing exercises.

Finally, only advanced climbers need bother with high-volume sport-specific training on fingerboards, ladders, campus or death boards, etc. Such climbers generally have finely tuned technique and need to partake of serious (potentially disastrous) training in an attempt to grasp the next higher level of climbing ability. In addition, you must get adequate rest and eat properly to fuel the effort required by a workout of this type.

A word on sports supplements: They vary in quality from pseudo-scientific hogwash to viable products. Still, they are no substitute for eating correctly. If you want an energy edge, I would recommend any good carbo fuel/energy drink that supplies complex carbs (from glucose polymers). The good ones will improve your endurance some by helping to maintain blood-glucose levels (the gasoline for climbing) through long workouts and days at the crags. Anything beyond that is up to you. Read up. And remember, these supplements are secondary to good, balanced grub, high in complex carbs and low in fat.

WEEK-END WARRIOR WORKOUT

Endless different routines are possible. The trick is how to schedule them; that is, when will you work out? There are now many sources from which a climber can learn and devise just what routine he or she will do pull-ups, hang board work, hand traversing, rope climbing, etc. The problem is, if you climb on weekends, it usually takes a day or two to recover, then it's already Wednesday. One schedule is to work out Monday and Thursday— Monday as hard as you can, and

Jody Rozin on the "Mutiny," (5.11d) Summersville Lake, New River Gorge, West Virginia.

Kevin Powell photo

Thursday moderately hard. It's hard to get up for a grueling workout after you've climbed yourself down to the quick the previous two days, but the Monday/Thursday schedule is good for overall results, leaving you sharp for the following Saturday.

The other option, and a favorite for those who disdain regular gym work, is to go bouldering (or indoor climbing) on Wednesday. This keeps you sharp, is a tremendous workout, and gives you two days' rest following both the weekend's toils and your mid-week efforts. If you're in good shape, you may try cragging on the weekends, then supplement your weekend work with a Tuesday/Thursday gym or bouldering routine. In the '70s, many of the hardest routes going up were accomplished by climbers following this very schedule: climb on Saturday and Sunday, back to work on Monday, sneak off on Tuesday and Thursday for an hour's late— afternoon bouldering, then back at it on the weekend.

In either case, make sure you milk your limited training time for all it's worth. Do this by focusing your efforts on working your weaknesses, not your strengths. Don't laugh— this tenet isn't as obvious nor as easy to adhere to as you think. Take Jim Bob for example. Jim can do 35 fingertip pull-ups and has the lock-off power of a hydraulic lift. He is also miserably inflexible. But because Jimmy doesn't want to look bad (and who does?) and his ego won't let him try something he isn't good at, he spends the majority of his training time whipping off pull-ups. Sure, he's gradually getting stronger, and his wing-like lats impress the ladies, but Jim is really wasting his time. If he simply devoted even half his workout to stretching he'd see an immediate and pronounced improvement on the rock. Hence, work at your weaknesses. It may not be fun, but it is the best way to use your precious time.

CIRCUIT TRAINING

The notion here is not to push yourself to muscular exhaustion, but to simply get some exercise. Therefore, it is possible to train a little each day, if you feel up to it. Precisely what your circuit will consist of is your call. Most comprehensive circuits involve various stations that give you a good overall pump, consisting on the whole of free-hand, or calisthenic-type movements— push-ups, sit-ups, dips, etc. This type of training is not particularly effective in building strength or power, but is excellent for overall conditioning. Remember that for optimum results, you should try and get your heart-beat over 120 beats per minute, and keep it there for at least 20 minutes.

Further Reference

Eric Hörst's excellent training books, part of this How to Rock Climb series, provide an expansion of the ideas presented here. They are *How to Climb 5.12,* a barebones program for fast performance improvement, and *Flash Training,* a detailed look at training processes and theory as they relate to rock climbing.

CHAPTER 10

Beta from the Experts

Slabs

Kevin Powell and Darrell Hensel are at the top of everyone's list; they were doing 5.12 slab and edging climbs nearly 20 years ago. Say Powell and Hensel:

"Tenuous testpieces and horrendous edging—this type of climbing, usually found on less than vertical rock, is where you will come to know the meaning of minute holds, tenuous positioning, and precise execution. First, let's talk about gear.

"Because precise footwork forms the basis of horrendous edging, don't skimp in obtaining the best possible footwear. Important features are harder rubber on the soles, lateral as well as longitudinal stiffness in the toe area and a close, tight fit overall. Any sloppiness in fit will allow the foot to slide and/or rotate inside the boot (during an edging move), greatly diminishing your ability and confidence when standing on minute holds. Experiment with different models on the boulders until you find just the right boot.

"Chalk should be chosen carefully. It should be somewhat coarse, without that "slick" feeling. Avoid the fine, powdery stuff. A stiff-bristled toothbrush is essential for cleaning holds and should be located (on the chalk bag) for quick and easy access.

"Other equipment needs will vary according to route and personal preference. What won't vary is the careful and calculated way in which you organize the gear. Rack up so you can easily and quickly access the gear with a minimum of fiddling in dicey situations. Remember, even the slightest annoyance or distraction can divert you from your goal.

"The techniques and intricacies of horrendous edging, though not easily mastered, can best be learned on the boulders. Thin-edge bouldering provides the best medium to experiment and refine your technique, and to develop and maintain the necessary finger calluses.

"The importance of how you hold on to edges cannot be overstated. When reaching for an edge, let your fingertips explore the edge's features and intricacies. Many holds, which at first feel marginal or even unusable, may feel considerably better with the slightest shifting of even one finger. So always shuffle your fingers over the whole edge. Make sure to get the thumb up to, or slightly over, the index finger. This substantially increases holding power and pulling force. Also, try to use only as much strength as is necessary to maintain your grip on the hold. Overcranking wastes energy and inevitably puts more holes in fingertips that press down

(opposite)

Suzanne Paulson on "Gorgeous," (5.10b) Owens River Gorge, California.

Kevin Powell photo

on razor-sharp edges. Hand and arm position also affect both the holding power and the way a hold feels; a slight change in their angle can make a hold feel much better or worse.

"To stand on, and rely on: Nowhere does this axiom prove more important than on horrendous edging problems. Effective use of the feet must be mastered. Precision is of the utmost importance. There are three basic positions in which the foot may be placed to obtain maximum advantage from an edge. The most common of these is true side-edging, where the part of the shoe between the ball of the foot and the point of the boot (along the edge of the big toe) is placed precisely on the edge. Make sure the heel is up and out so maximum force can be directed down and in onto the edge. This is the most versatile form of edging, allowing the most mobility, both vertically and laterally. This type of edging also allows you to compensate for the use of other types of footholds, and to maintain balance while putting together various sequences.

"Ball edging involves placing the edge of the boot at the ball of the foot precisely on the edge. This requires less toe strength and tends to be less strenuous on long, sustained edging problems. Its primary disadvantage is decreased sensitivity. It also puts your foot into a fixed position, providing very little mobility or chance for adjustment.

"Front pointing, which involves placing the point of the toe directly on the edge, proves most useful on bigger holds. This form of edging allows you to lean out more while you are climbing.

"The outside edge of the boot should not be forgotten as an option—though it can't be used on every route. The outside edge is particularly valuable when changing positions, say, from facing slightly left to facing slightly right. The ability to high step is no less valuable. A high step can allow you to use your feet even when the holds are few and far between. You can often avoid making a horrendous crank by stepping high enough to reach the next decent edge.

"Even if you plan carefully and use all of these techniques, you still occasionally will find yourself in that dreaded 'wrong foot' situation. When this happens, there are two possible solutions: Switch feet, or step through (jumping off isn't a viable option). When switching feet, you can support your weight by hanging on your fingers while moving one foot off the hold and placing the other onto it, or you can quickly shuffle one foot off, then the other foot on—sort of a controlled 'hop-step.' Either way, bear in mind that precision is the key here.

"If you choose to step through, you are again presented with a choice—stepping around in front, or behind, the set foot. No matter which way you step through, more caution is required than with the normal foot placement. You must pay careful attention to execution or you will force yourself out from and off the holds.

"When confronted with a baffling series of moves, you may find downclimbing (if possible) your most useful technique.

(opposite)

Ian Spencer-Green edging his way up a 13a somewhere in Utah.

Stewart M. Green photo

This gives you the ability to re-evaluate your sequence and overall strategy.

"Some things to avoid while using your feet:

Don't let your heel sag while standing on an edge;

• Don't overextend off your toe while reaching for the next hold;

• Try to keep your foot from moving on the edge.

"The above-mentioned actions greatly decrease your boot's holding power and inevitably lead to losing that point of contact. Bunching the feet close together also should be avoided as it usually results in unstable or out-of-balance positioning.

"A casual attitude is usually a poor strategy to bring to a horrendous edging route. Upon arriving at the base of the route, scout for any obvious features or weaknesses. Try to piece these together into some type of overall plan. Then, when you start climbing, make each move with calculated precision, making sure the move flows logically into the next one. If possible, try to conceive entire sequences that will get you from one rest hold to the next. However, don't get so locked into your approach or sequence that you can't improvise as needed. Two things are of primary importance: The ability to concentrate on what all four limbs are doing, and maintaining the right amount of force on each hold. Remember, above all, slab/edge climbing is an ongoing process of looking ahead, split-second decision making, and precise technical execution."

Let's listen to Bob Gaines, director of Vertical Adventures climbing school. Bob is a wizard on the slabs, and both his vast experience and 15 years of instructing have given him valuable insights. The following is excerpted from his fine treatise, *Slab Talk*:

"When I began rock climbing in the early 70s, the infamous "Stonemasters" ruled the Southern California crags. At that time, American and British climbers were setting the standards, and the Stonemasters were doing some of the hardest rock climbs in the world. Entrance into their elite clique was direct: You had to flash Valhalla, a 3-pitch face route at Suicide Rock, perhaps the first 5.11 edging climb in America. Back then, the best shoes were hard-rubber P.A.s and R.D.s, both totally unsuitable for difficult edging and smearing routes like Valhalla. Not until E.B.s came along did the ranks of the Stonemasters grow, though slightly.

"Everything changed when sticky rubber soles arrived. Precise edging was out and smearing was in—pasting the ball of the foot directly onto the rock, letting the edge, crystal or merest rugosity "bite" into the boot sole. Some climbers referred to this new technique as "smedging." Soon, even stickier rubbers appeared, and a slab renaissance ensued. Climbers ventured onto even blanker and steeper slabs. Some of the old test pieces were a full grade easier in the new boots, and by 1985, most every Suicide climber was a Stonemaster. Such is the part technology has played in slab climbing.

"Extreme slab climbing requires quick thinking to unravel puzzling move combinations. Exacting footwork is essential, as is balance and relaxation under duress. Even the slightest quaking will send the boot skating away.

"I like to work in two sets: handholds and footholds. First, I scan the rock for the two best handholds. On edges, I prefer the 'crimp' (placing the thumb over the forefinger) for optimal power. Digging the finger pads straight down onto the hold means positive purchase. When no obvious edges exist, simply digging the pads into the most roughly textured area will help. Many of the most extreme slab cruxes consist of sidepull combinations, pulling sideways on vertical edges with arms extended in an iron-cross position. On low-angle slabs, palming helps keep the center of gravity over the feet. The idea is—'nose over toes.' Novices are best taught the fundamentals of footwork and balance on low-angle slabs bereft of any handholds, forcing them to trust the friction of their boots while learning the subtleties of body position and center of gravity. Always visually follow the boot all the way to its placement on the hold. Never look up for a handhold until both feet are set. Watch a world-class climber and the first thing you'll notice is the fluid, ultra-precise footwork. Edges, sharp crystals and protruding rugosities are the most obvious smearing targets. On traverses, crossing inside with the opposite foot works best, using the outside portion of the boot that's crossing through to smear with. Ankle flexion helps maintain maximum surface contact between boot sole and rock. Always focus on shifting the center of gravity to directly above the ball of the foot you're stepping up on.

"On extreme slabs, where only the slightest dimples or ripples mar the slab plane, frontpointing on microsmears is called for. Here, just the very front tip of the boot is smeared, with the heel held relatively high. Temperature is key. Modern boot soles smear best at between 45° to 55° Fahrenheit, so take on that nasty pitch in the cool shade. Keep your boot soles meticulously clean. Rub off any dirt and grime and wash the soles if necessary (some climbers use rubbing alcohol to clean their soles). Once shod, never walk around in the dirt. The soles are never the same once dirt-impregnated. And never put chalk on your boot soles, as it greatly reduces your traction.

"The aspiring ace can benefit greatly from a long apprenticeship on the slabs. The subtle tricks of balance and footwork, well-learned through time on the rock, can be applied later to steeper test pieces where footwork still is key to success.

"For the expert, the extreme slab challenge demands a quick mind to solve the puzzle, mental poise and steady resolve for the long runouts, plus the exacting footwork and the balance of a dancer. Success at climbing what looks impossibly blank might just be the sweetest victory of all."

Rick Accomazzo is acknowledged as a master face climber and always has been particularly shrewd on the slabs.

Jeff Struthers frontpointing on micro-smears,
Squamish.

Tad Craig photo

Legendary for his composure in the face of chilling runouts, Rick climbs the blankest routes as though he were climbing stairs. In summary, let's find out why. Talk to us, Ricky:

"Slab climbing is the most subtle form of face climbing. At relatively low angles (roughly 45 to 70 degrees), difficult climbs make use of minute holds and fine variations in rock texture. It is this subtlety that provides one of the pleasures of climbing slabs. When you are climbing well, you can amaze yourself by moving over holds that are hardly perceptible. My first climbs were the slab routes of Tahquitz and Suicide Rock in California, and I still have a fondness for this type of climbing. Let me now pass on some advice gleaned from 19 years experience on slabs, experience gained from trial and error (i.e. by falling often).

"Good footwork is 75 percent of successful slab climbing. Because of the lesser angle, you can afford to be more deliberate than if you are racing against depletion of forearm reserves— which occurs on steeper face—and you need to be deliberate, for the footing is rarely positive, more often leaning toward the remarkably marginal. It's a contemplative sort of climbing that rewards finesse and balance rather than brute strength and endurance. Since falls are slower than on the vertical, and solid bolt protection often is used, runouts exceeding 20 feet are common. Consequently, to climb slabs well, one must have the ability and confidence to make marginal moves a long way out from the protection. For this, there is no secret: Practice is the only method by which climbers can become proficient and comfortable in the face of long falls. I can offer this tip: It is a natural tendency to tighten up and forget to breathe regularly when the last protection is receding at a disturbing pace and one becomes more and more aware of a long plunge. When I find my heart fluttering and my focus drifting to that last bolt, I stop, take a few slow breaths and try to marshal all my attention to the move at hand. I also make sure my center of gravity is away from the rock; that I have not unconsciously started leaning in, which is a sure prescription for a fall.

"It is more likely that your legs will tire and cause a misstep rather than your arms fatiguing, resulting in a failed grip. Thus, finding a periodic resting place for your feet is essential. Try to give your calves a break by standing on the outside edge of your boot, preferably on a good hold. A few moments on the outside edge can restore feeling to a numbed foot crammed into a snug boot. An even better respite is afforded by finding a hold big enough to stand on using the inside edge of the heel. This takes the pressure off the toes and the confidence tends to return with the blood flow. With practice, you can heel edge on fairly small holds and get a rest even in the midst of considerable difficulties.

"You must be in a good position to scrutinize the rock for the tiny slab nuances that can serve as holds. When looking down for potential footholds, it often helps to get your eyes close to the rock. From this attitude, you can see small differences in gradient or slight depressions or bumps that might offer purchase for your rock shoes. With your eyes close to the rock, the surface does not look nearly as featureless and flat, and you instantly become aware of more options than even a studied, straight-on look would afford.

"You must keep your weight over your feet. That is essential. The body (particularly the arse) must be kept as far as possible from the rock. This centers the weight over the feet and onto the shoes, ensuring maximum friction. Unfortunately, this position makes long reaches for handholds all the more perilous. As you reach, the hips draw closer to the rock and just as you attain that blue-ribbon nubbin, your feet will glide off, and down you go. I have seen many experienced climbers fall into this dilemma, which probably is the most common cause for slab falls. Better to make an intermediate step up, even if questionable, rather than try for that long reach.

"So, how do you keep your hips away from the rock, maintain the proper body position and still get a good look at potential footholds? Simply bend at the waist, place the top of your head against the rock and peer down from this position. The attitude forces the hips out and keeps maximum weight on the feet, while at the same time allowing a prime angle for spying footholds. While not the most dignified posture, it works wonderfully."

Steep Edging

Mari Gingery is one of the best and most experienced all-around climbers in the United States. Mari, along with Lynn Hill, first showed the rock climbing world that gender is no limitation. Those who feel otherwise are advised to watch her—and weep. Her vast experience runs from ghastly El Cap nail-ups to world-class free climbs. She is particularly magical on steep edging routes and the wisdom that follows helps to tell us why:

"First, note the temperature. Heat, humidity, and direct sunlight can make a hard-edging climb horrendous. Wait for the shade and hope for a breeze to help keep your fingertips from pouring sweat. Your shoes should be relatively stiff with good (read "not trashed") edges, but with enough flexibility to feel the rock through the soles. They should fit like a second skin, particularly forward of your arch. You don't want your foot rolling inside the shoe during a difficult edging move. Some climbers swear by plank-like boots, others by super-tight, lace-up slippers. I prefer a moderately-designed boot suitable for my specific weight. The heavier climber may desire a more substantial shoe. Regardless, the steeper the edging, the better a stiff boot works. Since difficult edging concentrates most of your weight on a very small portion of your foot, a relatively comfortable fit is best. Lace snugly, but not painfully.

"Jitters and slapdash maneuvering lead to uncontrollable leg tremors and peelers. Before you start climbing, take a moment to calm your mind and focus your attention. A relaxed and confident attitude increases both your enjoyment and chances of success.

"Once collected and focused, scan the route for the line of least resistance to the first good stance. Mentally chart the best holds and plan a sequence that will most easily gain you a solid position. Hard-edging routes resemble climbing a convoluted ladder—with very small rungs, of course—but nevertheless a continuous series of steps. Consider your hands as points of balance and the means to direct body movement as you step from foothold to foothold. Only when the footholds become marginal do the hands increase their load-bearing. The quickest way to burn out is to simply pull yourself from hold to hold, dragging your carcass behind. The notion is to expend the least amount of energy necessary to progress upwards. You'll have to divide your weight between your arms and legs, but always keep as much weight as possible over your feet.

"Precise foot placement is key on difficult edging because your point of contact is so minimal. Learn to place your boot accurately; if you need to shift your weight, do so until you can feel positive contact with the rock. Test what you can and cannot do on the boulders. Learn to trust your feet when you're on a sharp edge, and discover just how much weight you can place on a dime edge without popping off. Experiment to determine how you can achieve the most positive contact with the rock. Try standing on various points, from your big toe to the ball of your foot. Try the outside edge as well, the very toe, the heel—everywhere. Rotate your ankle to get the most boot rubber on the edge. Turning your foot sideways, parallel to the face, allows more of your edge to contact the rock, but also requires substantial hip "turnout" to feel comfortable. Different climbers prefer different foot positions, so experiment to discover what works best for you.

"While clinging hard to handholds instills a greater feeling of security, knowing where your feet are usually is more crucial. Also, to conserve hand strength (and fingertips), don't overgrip. Hold on just hard enough to stay put.

"Crimping—lining up your fingertips on an edge and locking your thumb over your index finger—normally gives the best grip. But watch this technique—too much crimping can trash your fingers. To find the most positive grip, feel around the edge and adjust your fingers over the subtle irregularities. Find the best placement before you pull on it. Sometimes even a minor adjustment can give a marginal hold a much surer feel.

Ian Spencer-Green on
"Je suis un Legende,"
Verdon Gorge, France.

Stewart M. Green photo

"As you climb, carefully placing your feet on edges, concentrate on a smooth weight transfer from one foot to another. The legs supply the push; the hands direct your motion
and give secondary support that is relative to how thin the
footholds are. Maintain your balance with at least two, preferably three, points of support; two handholds and a foothold,
or two footholds and a handhold. Move one limb at a time. As

you move up, try to keep your center of gravity between your points of contact. For example, when traversing, you can counterbalance a leftward lean by extending your right leg out to the right. This also situates your weight and balance over your left foot—which is edging—and precludes the need to hang from an arm. For traversing sections, use cross-overs (one hand over or under the other) and step-throughs (inside or outside your supporting foot) to set up a reach to one side or the other. Shuffling hands and feet works, but often adds unnecessary moves. Hand and foot switches are tricky, but can be made more manageable by planning to leave space for the second hand or foot. A slick hand switch is to lift one or two fingers off a hold and replace them with fingers from the other hand. Foot switches can be executed as a well-timed hop-and-switch—which quickly can become an untimely hop-and-pop if poorly performed. When footholds are awkwardly spaced, consider taking several small steps to set up your foot position, rather than a single large step. Never rule out an extremely high step. Such a move can take the bite out of an otherwise thin crank by establishing a high foothold, which allows the leg, rather than the fingertips, to propel you up. Stout feet and calves help to maintain solid edging position without fatigue; strong thighs and gams help to leg out those high steps.

"Resting techniques, including very brief rest stops, are essential. You need time to look and think without exhausting your fingers. Good-sized edges provide obvious resting points. Stemming between footholds also lets you shake out and take a breather. Anytime you can get most of your weight over your feet for more than a few seconds is time for rest. Taking brief breathers throughout a long section is a way to extend your stamina. After a high step, sitting on your heel is a stable, static, but temporary position from which you momentarily can get off your fingertips and scope the next moves. Use every chance to get off your arms and save your finger strength, as that will greatly extend the time you have to contemplate the next sequence. Pace yourself.

"Edging sequences often are devious and difficult to perceive quickly. To conserve strength, scan and evaluate upcoming moves from a rest point, then move quickly over the small footholds and thin pulls to the next relatively good stance. Linger briefly at relatively large holds to cool your fingertips and plot a course through the following section. Eye the route carefully, looking for obvious (and obscure) flakes and edges, points of protection, and route meanderings. Visualize the sequence of moves that will lead to the next stance. If there is an obvious point on a route where a particular hand is required on a hold (i.e., where a route moves abruptly sideways), think backwards down the handholds and determine which hand will start you off on the correct sequence. As you begin a difficult section, move quickly and smoothly. Keep looking around—especially down—for holds you may have overlooked. Keep a 'flow' of motion going until you reach the next stance. Don't think about any particular technique or tricks. Let your mind translate the pattern of holds into fluid motions. Experience will help you recognize shapes and patterns of holds and respond with appropriate moves. Strive for control. Be precise with your footwork. When you reach a point of uncertainty, it often is helpful to climb up a few moves and look around, get an idea of a probable sequence then downclimb back to a stance to regroup before tackling the crux. Downclimbing from a puzzling section gives you time to feel out the holds, consider your sequence and recover somewhat before launching out again.

"Having linked handholds and footholds together into moves, and moves into sequences, you should think about clipping into some protection. Be sure your gear is organized and easily accessible before you leave the ground. Carry only what you will need, but be sure you have enough gear to gain the belay and clip yourself in. Many edging routes are bolt-protected and require only the use of carabiners. Normally, climbers clip into a bolt with a quickdraw but a single locking carabiner also can be used to minimize a fall or ensure that the rope does not come unclipped. Good stances typically are found at each bolt, and these are secure places to rest and evaluate the remaining moves. Putting all of this information together with some imagination and desire should enable you to clip into the anchor bolts on your route.

"Thin-hold climbing is a tenuous type of ascent favoring balance, precision, and control over raw strength. However, the honed footwork and balanced, controlled form acquired on difficult edging routes will help you climb steeper, more strenuous routes."

Steep Face Climbing

Christian Griffith has forged himself an international reputation for scaling some of the hardest steep face climbs from France to Colorado. Says Christian:

"Some of the world's most classic and historical routes are vertical face climbs. On no other angle does the coordination of a climber's limbs, as well as the integration of different kinds of movement, play such a significant role in ascent. Also, vertical face climbs serve as the best training ground for the latest vogue of overhanging testpieces.

"An even distribution of weight on both hands and legs is essential. Precision on reaches often is measured in millimeters. Body tension and the conservation of energy are paramount for success. Only on vertical rock can all of these elements be learned.

"When on particularly scant holds, think of each individual move as having two parts: anticipation and execution. Every move, big or small, alters your balance point. You must anticipate this, and adjust by shifting your weight. This is best accomplished with hip movement, sometimes exaggerated. Whatever the extent of hip movement, the point is to climb deliberately. Anticipating and adjusting before a move helps

eliminate any swaying or jiggling once you start cranking.

'Turn-ou' is a tricky concept, and refers to the hip's proximity to the rock in relation to the relative height of the feet. Perfect turn-out would find a climber's butt as low as his heels, while having the knees splayed out and hips pressed against the wall. Turn-out facilitates lateral and vertical mobility, while allowing the feet to absorb maximum weight. Getting used to the concept of turn-out—which essentially refers to the ability to open up your hips—best can be learned on the slabs. Again, the idea is to keep your butt as close to your heels as possible, while keeping your hips close to the rock. You will not always want to climb in this squat posture, but it is an invaluable technique when the need arises.

"A crucial technique is the 'dead point.' I refer here to a short form of dynamic that permits long reaches when a lack of power or an awkward stance make a static reach impossible. An all-out dynamic will sometimes span four feet of rock; a powerglide is a lesser form of the all-out dyno; a dead point, however, rarely exceeds an arm's length in distance. While the all-out dynamic primarily is a matter of generating and controlling upward locomotion, a dead point emphasizes the body's inward movement. In short, we can dynamically suck our body toward the rock, and at the moment when we're weightless—the dead point—we can flash a hand up to the desired hold. Remember, the closer you are to the rock, the more extension you have off your feet and the higher your reach.

"Dead points often are performed off the most minuscule holds. The execution must be precise, and for the split second at the dead point, when your torso has been drawn to the rock and your hand flashes up for the next hold, your body must remain absolutely still. Once you clasp the hold, you'll make small and instantaneous adjustments that allow you to hang on. Again, try to anticipate the play of your balance point so that when you do reach, your position is the most comfortable one that can be held unwaveringly until latching that next hold. Accuracy and timing are key. Remember not to direct your dynamic energy exclusively upward, as you would in an all-out dynamo, but diagonally up and in. A quick, strong pop with the hips is the best way to initiate this motion, particularly if the handholds are small.

"It is common for climbers to think of their hands only as a set of fingers, and to consider only the front soles of their boots. Correct modes of conserving strength and enhancing power requires some rethinking of these concepts. By using my thumbs, I can greatly increase my holding power. Sometimes, rather than wrapping my thumb over my index finger, as in a crimp, I will place my thumb directly on a hold, then wrap my fingers over the thumb. This will limit your range of motion in certain instances, but when the situation is right—with both straight pulls and hangs—this thumb technique can boost my power some 50%.

"On bigger holds, notably knobs and horns, I often wrap

(opposite)

Christian Griffith in Eldorado Canyon, Colorado.

Beth Wald photo

the heel of my hand over them. This sometimes gives me a much better grip than I would get by clasping the same hold with my fingers. A limited technique, yes, but I have found it a very effective way to rest my forearms, particularly during competition climbing.

"You'll often see people using their feet as stumps, as though they've lost all sensation from the big toe back. Granted, the bulk of your footwork takes place between the arch and the big toe, but the rear part of the foot also has utility. On several desperate routes, I found that by high-stepping directly onto my heel I attained faster and better balance than had I stood on the ball of my foot. This heel technique is rarely used, but is a good trick for getting a quick reach, or grabbing a moment's rest.

"I've also found that using slippers has greatly increased my foot awareness. Slippers allow you to use your feet like your hands, as their supple form curls over the edges and actually pulls you into the rock.

"Climbing is no dance. You need ballet-like precision in the midst of extreme physical effort, but there is nothing artfully contrived in vertical face climbing. Success hangs on efficiency and conserving energy. Styles amongst top climbers vary from fluid to mechanical, but the goal always is to move one part of the body while making minimum demands on the rest. Maintaining a balance of energy on the limbs is crucial, and disrupting this equilibrium—often measured in ounces— can fumble a dead point or send your foot off a key hold. Kinesthetic sense results in consistency, consistency in success."

Overhanging Face Climbing

As we've seen in previous chapters, overhanging face climbing is as much a matter of technique as sheer strength. To help flesh out our understanding of the techniques involved, let's listen to international speed climbing champion, Hans Florine, who spends more time upside down than otherwise.

"No one is strong enough to hang out on their arms all day. You've got to read the moves and execute them decisively. With on-sight climbing, when you hope to do the route on your first try, you must have faith both in the accuracy of the rating (of that route), and your ability to flash it. If you're on a 5.8 route that's well within your limit, but find yourself pumped out, you usually can pull up, lock off, reach around above, and most likely your hand will slip into a pocket or onto a jug big enough for you to carry on. The most common disclaimer you'll hear about overhanging routes is: 'I would have made it had I seen that hold a second earlier.' Often on overhanging rock, you can't see a hold, especially a pocket, until you've pulled up to it, or even past it.

"Body position is key to conserving energy and strength on overhanging rock. You've got to keep your arms straight when resting, or trying to rest. When moving up, try to avoid locking off the holds. Move up by pushing with your legs and

rotating your arms using your shoulders. You'll quickly pump out if you just crank up the route bent-armed, as you would climb a Bachar ladder. By working your feet up and rotating your shoulders like clock arms, it's possible to bring a side pull from over your head all the way to your stomach without ever bending your elbow. Often, backstepping one foot can

Bobbi Bensman on "Vitamin H," 12c/d, Rifle, Colorado.

Stewart M. Green photo

twist your torso closer to the rock, allowing you to rotate up on one arm with far less effort.

"You'll do a lot of toe pointing on overhanging routes, so a low-top shoe is recommended."

Scott "Coz" Cosgrove is a low-profile climber who has established some of the hardest routes in the United States. A demon on the overhangs, Scott adds these valuable insights:

"Concentration, fluid breathing, simplicity of movement, sequence memory, and a do -or- die tenacity for hard flashes are your basic ammo for overhanging climbing. Advanced routes further require the precision footwork of a high-wire walker, the rhythm and loose hips of M.C. Hammer, and the ability to snatch holds like a frog tongues its prey.

"Many times what holds you onto the overhang is the counter-pressure of opposing hands and feet— i.e., right hand pulling, left foot hooked, and vice versa. Remember that most toe and heel hooks are much more secure when you pull a little with the leg. Keep an eye out for hooks, but don't waste time and energy trying to have both feet set all of the time. Dangling a foot actually can help stabilize you. If opposing hand and foot placement is impossible, try crooking your free foot and leg under your planted foot to correct your balance.

"Learning to dyno is hard, but two tricks have helped the Coz. First, always try to latch the lunged-for hold at your dead point. Second, focus your concentration and energy on your thrusting handholds: your 'power point.' For super-long dynos, you might have to keep your head down at the start of the lunge, then look up and grab the hold while in flight. Focusing on the hold at the start makes aiming easier, but the upright head adversely affects your balance and cuts your vector, resulting in limited height. This peek-a-boo dyno requires plenty of practice to master, however.

"Resting and simplifying moves are much the same thing. Your arms have limited fuel, so don't waste it with unnecessary lock-offs, fancy footwork or climbing with bent arms or crooked shoulders. I find that hanging from holds with open palms is less strenuous than crimping. Crimping, like slow, static movement, should be used only when necessary. Climb like an inchworm. Place your hands and bring your feet up in one motion, thrust up to the next holds and, whenever possible, latch with open palms (open grip) and straight arms, then bring the feet up immediately and repeat the process.

"When resting on holds, I count to 30, resting each limb in turn. Depending on the holds, I'll sometimes repeat the process two or three times, concentrating on pumping the blood back into my arms. Knowing when to rest and when to pump it out is crucial; only experience can tell you when and where to try and recover, and when to keep on keeping on.

"You need a relaxed mind when the going gets rugged, and this is impossible without maintaining controlled, natural breathing. The best climbers never hold their breath, though this is common with novices. To maximize that relaxed attitude, breathe deep and hold each breath for a half-second; then exhale fully, blowing out carbon dioxide and thinning the lactic acid—the burn—in your limbs.

"Since rhythm and looseness are a must, I lug a boom-box to the cliff, plug in a little Motown and keep it cranking till I'm into my groove. Go with familiar tunes to keep your concentration. Best results come when you don't tie your personal happiness to success or failure on a route. If you ever approach a route with a climb-it-at-all-costs attitude, you've made yourself a slave to success, which creates undo pressure and torpedoes your ability to relax, focus, and, above all, enjoy yourself. Relax, crank hard, and turn anxiety into raw power.

"Finally, leave the hemp and booze at the pad. Better yet, pitch them into the dumpster. You need a clear mind to analyze and execute your line. When I try to flash a route, I climb it many times in my mind, conceiving two or three probable strategies. To do this, I need a clear mind, not one addled by drug or drink.

"Climbing overhangs is in itself the best practice. Try to learn one thing at a time, instead of baffling yourself with information overload. Move quickly and naturally, stay loose and focused. Good luck!"

Russ Walling is an ace climber who disdains anything but steep routes. Some of his philosophies differ considerably from those of other climbers. To get another opinion, let's listen to Russ:

"Paddling around on the slabs is good fun for you and your date, but the steep stuff is where it all happens. Once the angle and severity increase, so do the demands on the climber. Picture a climber on a 120° wall, dangling from an eighth-inch acorn, one foot epoxied to an atom-sized nubbin, struggling with a desperate clip. That is no slouch up there, rather a highly specialized athlete. He probably tips the scales at about 123 pounds wringing wet, but his mitts are like vice locks. Yes, world-class strength is a good friend to have, but sharp technique has landed countless more climbers at the top of big-number testpieces than power alone.

"You need experience, and you'll only find that on overhanging rock. However, said rock need not be desperate or committing. The boulders are the ultimate training ground for building up a library of moves directly applicable to overhanging routes. Rock is rock. Every hold you grab can teach you something about balance, personal limits, and methods. Bouldering is invaluable because some of the best routes are little more than boulder problems found in the middle of a pitch.

"Every hold has a best way to grasp it. Use it wrong and you're off. Use it right and you're rewarded with another hold just as demanding. Link the series of holds perfectly and the summit is yours. The key is to find what feels most positive on the hold, then forget about it and begin to pull. Much energy is wasted fretting over a handhold, milking it, then, with fail-

Bobbi Bensman climbing at Rifle, Colorado.

Beth Wald photo

ing strength, trying to pull on something that now feels crappy. Pop! You're gone. If you simply had grabbed the hold, clasped the best part and pulled through, chances are you'd be on your way to the summit instead of hanging in your harness, bitching about how greased the hold was. You made it greasy with all the cocking around. Grab it and move.

"When you're satisfied that your hand has found the optimum grip, the pulling begins. If you're climbing statically, it's usually straightforward. You seek out holds above, then pull the hold down to around your pec, lock it off, and repeat the process. It is important not to change the angle of your hand once you've clasped the hold. If it feels good with your wrist low and near the rock, keep it there. When your hand angle changes relative to the rock, so does the force on your fingers, and that often makes the hold less positive.

"Each pull with your arms should be complimented by thrust with your legs. Push, pull, lock off, reach and fluidly repeat the process. You're wasting energy if you're pulling up, locking off, then trying to land your feet somewhere. Combined use of hands and feet will keep enough gas in your tank to allow a peek at the summit.

"On overhanging rock, footwork has been taken to a fine art. Every boot manufacturer offers some sort of precision-fitted, helium-weighted, drooped-toe, Ginsu-soled, atomic ballerina, big-name climber Signature Model climbing shoe. All the hype does actually aid the name of the game—footwork.

Each foothold has a best spot on which to stand. Most often, you place your toe or heel on overhanging rock, but be creative and never rule out the unorthodox— the outside edge, the instep, anything that works. Again, the key is to find it, set it, and move on. If it sticks, you're a hero. If you keep fretting over it, pawing endlessly at the face for exemplary purchase, you're as good as through. And just because it's a foothold doesn't mean it will be found at your feet. If you visit Hueco Tanks, for instance, heel hooks located over your head are your saviors. Think of hanging on a pull-up bar above a pool of hungry gators. Which would you rather have? Greasy palms and them gators nipping at your heels, or a leg up over the bar as you taunt Wally with a free hand. Point is, anytime you can take weight off your arms, do so!"

Whether the inimitable John Sherman ("Vermin") is known better as a fabulous climber or an addled curmudgeon is debatable. For a decade, his articles have informed, entertained, and frequently revolted the American climbing audience. Says John:

"Overhangs force weight onto the arms, and even with quick movement, one's arms can swell like dirigibles. Without good footwork, creative resting, and extensive training, the result can be Hindenbergian. So, the most important thing is to keep as much weight over the feet as possible. Keeping your feet on an overhanging wall requires great abdominal strength. When only one foot is on the rock, the dangling leg should be used as a counterbalance and often assumes radical, magazine-ad positioning. "High footholds often are a good choice. They are easier to reach—provided you have the flexibility—and provide a support point closer to your center of gravity. On overhangs under 120°, one sometimes can place a foot on a positive, waist-high hold, then sit on the heel, much like the rest position aid climbers use in etriers. This takes a lot of weight off the guns and allows the use of Lilliputian handholds.

"On overhangs beyond 120°, heel hooking is often used. These hooks work best when the heel is above your center of gravity. Frequently, a heel is hooked above the hands. Try to get as much weight as possible on the heel, and if a heel-toe jam can be found, so much the better ("sticky" rands are a boon here). Heel hooking below one's center of gravity is effective when the hook is secure enough to pull outward from the wall. This taxes the hamstrings, but can provide an effect similar to the high foothold/aid climber's rest.

"Even with footwork like Fred Astaire, one's arms still will have to support some weight. This is best managed with straight arms. With the skeletal system bearing the weight, only hand and forearm strength is needed to hang on. Expert climbers actually can rest in this straight-armed attitude, shaking out until they regain sufficient gusto to move on. When moving, remember to let the legs push the body up, using the arms only to keep the torso close enough to the wall to reach the next hold. When the holds are well spaced, using straight arms is, of course, impossible. If the footholds are there, go with a full lock-off, with hand next to shoulder, and chest sucked into the wall. Any arm position between straight and full lock-off quickly will gobble up your strength (a few seconds experimenting on a pull-up bar will verify this). Move fast in these situations.

"Body twists can allow long reaches on severely over-hanging rock while keeping the arms straight. By twisting the upper body so that the shoulder axis becomes perpendicular to the rock, the hand supporting the climber's weight ends up low—below the opposite armpit, or lower still. This support-ing arm remains straight and crosses the chest and stomach. The reaching arm can be extended now, in a line parallel to the supporting arm, to reach the next hold. This technique utilizes the trunk muscles. Good holds are a must. On rare occasions, dire circumstances or the urge to show-off forces one to climb on the arms alone. Here, use both arms to pull up, only releasing one when grasping the next hold. 'Kipping'—a deliberate and often natural pulling up of the knees—can help establish upward thrust while kicking the gut muscles in to assist the lats, shoulders, and guns.

"When the arm's hydraulics aren't up to statically cranking a move, lunging comes into play. "Dead point" refers both to the space between a sportclimber's ears, and the apex of his lunge, when the body is momentarily weightless. That's when you'll want to grab the lunged-for hold. Often, climbers will opt for dynamic moves over static ones, so they can move faster and conserve energy. When lunging, let the legs do as much of the work as possible. Think of the hands only as a pivot point about which the body will rotate up to the next hold. Set the feet well, sink low, then push with the legs. Let's not see any of this one, two, three, pumping-up-and-down jive before lunging. This just wastes energy and pumps up one's doubts. Sink down once and go!

"With the exception of wide cracks and employment, most climbers find roofs the most intimidating obstacles they come across. Arms remain straight as they usually don't have to pull up. Sticking under a roof (especially keeping the feet on) usually involves opposition techniques. Resting is usually impossible, so move fast.

'Wasn't that roof easy?' Now you're at the lip, a thousand meters of bowel-loosening air beneath you—and the next six feet look bleak. Turning any lip is rough duty because the body hinges at the waist and the legs feel as though a Waimea undertow is sucking them back under the roof. Depending on the holds, surmounting said lip can involve a straight-on man-tel, rocking over a foot hooked on the very lip, dragging one-self over on guns alone—even hucking a free-hanging, Clark Kent-dynamic for a higher hold. Whatever, getting the hips over the lip is critical and is most easily done with the hands as high above the lip as possible.

"Resting is key on long overhangs. (Unending endurance will only get you so far—five-figure contracts, etc.) Plan rests in advance by surveying the line and picking spots where you can see a possible rest. On overhangs these spots will be jugs, jams, knee bars, and over-the-head footlocks. Knee bars are the best bet for a no-hands rest on overhanging turf.

"Training for overhanging face climbing is best done on the boulders—technique and power are readily acquired there. Long traverses are tedious, but effective for building endurance. It's wrist curls in the gym that build Sherman-esque forearm endurance. The forearms always are first to go. Forget the finger boards, they just promote injury. A King Kong upper body will help on power moves, but might screw you when it comes to endurance and is no substitute for technique.

"Let the legs do the work, keep the arms straight, move fast, plan rests in advance, and don't ever give up!"

Arêtes

Few climbers have taken up arêtes as a special study. One of those is Orlando Vitalis. Orlando's sage advice is "must" reading for anyone interested in tackling the more exacting arêtes, a specie of route popping up more frequently than ever.

"Something to consider before starting out is on which side you should rack your gear. Many times, the climbing will take place on one side of the edge, leaving only one hand free to place the gear (on difficult arêtes, two-handed rests are unheard-of). Other times, climbing around the corner is required, making placement more thought-and pump-provoking. Often you can figure out from the deck what side you'll predominantly be climbing on. So take your time, and inspect the route carefully from below.

"Arêtes usually are strenuous, so the key is to figure out the best sequence and execute it quickly, but with control. Once you start climbing, move fluidly. Constantly look and feel around the corner for hidden holds. If holds allow, it's often more efficient to switch sides for 10 feet, versus liebacking straight up the edge. Remember, there are two planes to climb on, so remain aware of each of them. Many times, the easiest sequence is obscure and improbable-looking.

"Hesitating or hanging about can throw you off balance and instantly pump you out. Unless you easily can let go with one or both hands, all but short rests are ill-advised: they're probably 'sucker' rests, which only waste time and valuable energy. It's almost always better to keep moving.

"Heel, toe, and calf hooks are invaluable aids to maintain balance, limit the 'hinge' effect, and, at least briefly, unweight your arms. Many arêtes are impossible without using these techniques. A tiny indentation on the blind side of the arête can feel like a jug when your heel is hooked on it properly. So keep track of what your hands already have passed over—it might save you from barn-dooring off. Often, a hook can provide a quick rest to shake out an arm. On one first ascent I did—the incomparable Magnetic Pork—I was able to place a

left heel hook above my left hand, which enabled me to move the left hand up statically, thus avoiding a desperate dyno-slap. The move was possible without the high heel hook, but was twice as strenuous and so fried my bacon that, once done, I couldn't flash the climbing above. The heel hook was the key.

"Slapping most often is necessary to pass blank sections between holds. It also is useful when gravity and body position require you to hold on with both hands, but you must slap and latch before pitching off. Be aggressive and quick whenever you slap. Don't overcling, which will produce an insta-pump but don't slap casually, either, because that can send you winging into space. Slapping is a dynamic maneuver, and you must make use of the dead point—that millisecond when your body is weightless. Preceding any slap, you (usually) must dynamically hoist your torso up and slightly in. At the dead point, a hand flashes up for the hold. Perfect timing is the key here, just like with hitting a baseball.

"On extreme arêtes, body position is critical for conservation of energy. Muscles not being used should be relaxed, but ready to spring. Relaxing muscles and conserving energy often means the difference between the summit and flight time. Use body position to your advantage. On steep and overhanging routes, keep your center of gravity (your hips) close to the wall and never try to force, or 'muscle,' your way up.

"Sometimes, you won't be able to stop and chalk up because your clutch on the arête is too desperate. In this case, even the slightest wind can help keep your hands dry. Also, be aware of humidity, which can make hands sweaty. Colder weather is ideal for climbing arêtes. Skin and rubber friction increase dramatically when the temperature is below 55°.

"The multi-dimensional nature of arête climbing provides exciting combinations of moves and intriguing problem-solving designs, both mental and physical. Good luck fighting the pump!"

Rope Tricks for Sport Climbing

Sport climbing puts the highest premium on sheer difficulty. Most every sport climb is a "clip-and-go" route: bolted from bottom-to-top, and relatively—if not positively—safe, but often desperate to actually climb. The harder the route is—the closer it approaches your technical limit—the less probable it is that you can climb it on your first try, or even your first day of trying. To hasten the process, various rope shenanigans have been devised. Though these tricks involve a lot of dangling and hanging about, and are essentially quasi-direct aid techniques, they all are geared to the desired end of a clean, free ascent, and can get you there much faster than going about your work in a traditional manner. Ace free climber Christian Griffith has supplied us with the following counsel:

'Rope tricks' are invaluable skills for modern free climb-

(opposite)

Ian Spencer-Green on "Bite the Blue Sky," 12d, Penitente Canyon, Colorado.

Stewart M. Green photo

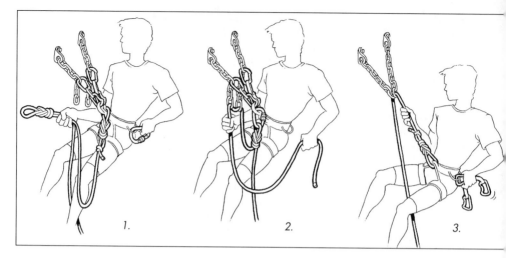

1.   2.   3.

Changing over at a
hanging anchor:

Changing over at a hanging anchor:

1. Clip into the anchors directly with quickdraws. (Don't loop into any chain that may connect the bolts; if one bolt fails your tie would fail). Tie a figure-eight loop in the rope.

2. Clip the figure-eight directly into your harness, untie from the rope, and pass the end through the end of the anchor chains.

3. Tie the end of the rope directly into your harness again, with a back up knot, have your belayer support you on the new tie-in, unclip your quickdraw tie-ins, and lower away.

ing. Techniques like 'hang-dogging' and 'springing,' essential to efficiently 'work' a route, were originally shunned because of their resemblance to aid climbing techniques. To avoid confusion, think of rope tricks as a means—and never a substitute—for the subsequent free ascent. What is the desired end is a perfectly clean free ascent, bottom-to-top, with no falls and no hanging.

"Rope tricks are tools of the trade, and as with any trade, the work involved in learning a route requires that you first decide which tricks are most useful. As a general rule, if there is any shadow of a chance that you might be able to flash the route without any previous information (on-sight), go for it! You have only one on-sight try on a given route per lifetime, so don't throw it away. Overextending yourself on a safe sport route can only help you understand where your natural limits lie, and a good, whole-hearted 'burn' is always worth it.

"Once you have ascertained that the route is hard enough to use tricks on, forget about free climbing for a while, and become an aid climber. The easiest solution is to simply rig a toprope, and take it from there. Exploiting a toprope is pretty self-explanatory—you can hang for rests and to inspect the moves, tension over hard moves, try one move at a time, or handwalk back up a few moves. Whatever works. However, in many cases a toprope is either impossible to rig, or is impractical, so you must work from the ground up. This is where the more involved rope tricks come into play.

"If you know where the crux is, and you have reason to believe it will be quite hard for you, use the fastest means to get up there you can. Pull on bolts, take tension from the rope, or use a trick Scott Franklin showed me: Clip three quickdraws together to fashion a short aid sling. Use this wherever you can to conserve as much energy as possible until you gain the crux section. Once there, rest for awhile before trying the moves. Study the holds, and try to piece together a viable sequence before you start cranking. Since that trick affords the fastest and least strenuous way to get to the crux, you should be able to ascertain pretty quickly if the route is even possible for you. If you can't boulder out the crux, having hung on the bolt, studied and rehearsed it, it is foolish to think you will be able to climb it after legitimately climbing up to that spot, sans hanging and resting. If the moves don't go quickly, but you think you have a chance, frig your way (hang, aid climb, whatever) to the next bolt, and drop back down with a toprope to inspect all the subtleties of the sequence. Try to climb it on tension—a lot at first, less later, and finally none at all. If the sequence seems impossible, break it down to individual moves, then start linking them together until you can do the whole sequence. Rest, and do it again and again, until you've got it wired and can look forward to cranking it off on the lead, rather than fearing it all the way up the lower section. If you simply cannot crank the moves, though they seem not so far beyond you, retire to the boulders and try to find a few problems that replicate the moves in whole or part. Look for similar holds, angles of pull and torque, body position and balance, and do these problems countless times until your body is dialed into the program. Then return to the route.

"After you've worked the crux, drop down and work the moves below the crux. If you have climbed 'bolt-to-bolt' up to the crux, that is, if you have done all the actual moves below, but have rested on the bolts all the way up, don't feel assured you can 'dick' the route without hanging. It's a little like running the mile in hundred-yard spurts. When you try to link the parts together, the proposition is a very different one. Climbing bolt-to-bolt does give a leader certain invaluable insights, however. Take special care to memorize any rests or potential shake-outs. Many great climbers have squandered their power and have consequently spent extra days on routes with moves they have perfectly rehearsed, but with rests and shakes they have neglected to learn. Equally important is to learn how and where to clip the bolts. Practice this in mime on the toprope. Discover and practice the body position from which the clip is least strenuous, and don't waste strength on physically 'making' the clips. Again, much of this can be rehearsed with tension, until you have worked out what works best for you. On routes that are at your physical limit, you must execute a long and involved sequence perfectly if you're to succeed. One false clip, missed shake, or fumbled move, and you're off.

"Overhanging rock requires special rope tricks. A classic example is 'springing.' Say a climber has fallen far enough below the last bolt that he can't reach back in to the belay rope—in other words, he's left dangling in space. If he wants to regain the high point without lowering off and re-climbing the lower section, he or she can 'spring' back up to the highest bolt with the help of a skilled and stout belayer. To spring, the climber must pull up as high as he can on the rope, while the belayer leans his weight back against the belayed line, now taut as a harpstring. The climber then releases his grip,

Brett Spencer-Green on "Child of Light," 13d, Enchanted Tower, New Mexico.

Stewart M. Green photo

producing a mini-fall, during which the modicum of slack produced is in part taken up by the belayer, who falls back until he shock-loads the line. The belayer then locks the belay off, moves back to the original position, ready to absorb the slack of another spring if necessary, and so on. The procedure is repeated until the leader is within reach of the rope running back down to the belayer, whence he can pull himself back up the remaining distance to the top, clipped bolt. However, this technique can produce severe loading on the rope and the highest point it passes through. If you are using 'cold shut' top rope anchors, you definitely don't want to employ springing. Cold shuts are the large hangers that are formed by bending a steel rod into a hook or closed 'eye.' Because they are not nearly as strong as standard bolt hangers, the rope can deform them. Never practice springing on a hook-shaped cold shut—the rope could easily jump out.

"Another technique for overhanging rock is 'down-jumping.' Down-jumping allows you to practice lower moves on a route where you've already nailed the crux. Toproping from the bolt above the crux is impossible because when you pitch, you'll be so far out in space you won't be able to pull back into the rock. Each section must therefore be worked from the bolt closest to it (above it). If the rope is clipped off too high, you'll be left dangling every time you pitch off. You're essentially working from the top down. Unclip from the bolt, and try to downclimb until you pop, or better yet, warn your belayer, and have him forcefully suck in slack as he pulls you off. This technique saves you from falling further than you need to, and eliminates wasting time and energy pulling or springing back up to the bolt you just fell onto. Because of the proliferation of bolts on most sport climbs, we are rarely talking about falling more than a body length. Remember, however, that it is these short, wrenching falls that most stress both the rope and the bolts, so special attention should be directed to both. Likewise, the belayer should be well-versed in his craft. With too big a discrepancy in weight between the climber and belayer, things can get problematic. Ideally, you'll want a rather portly belayer who is nimble on his feet. The whole business takes practice—and remember, it's the action of the belayer falling back that takes in the slack. Even the quickest hands cannot draw in slack through a belay device. It's best to keep the rope locked off altogether. Either way, these procedures cause premature wear on all the gear, which should be retired long before the normal time.

"Once the better part of the moves, rests and clips have been figured out, familiarize yourself with the climbing after the crux. I prefer to work this section last, because on a successful red point attempt, it is precisely this last section where I will be most gassed. Therefore I want this section to be freshest in my memory. Remember that no matter how easy the closing moves of a route may be—learn them. There is nothing more frustrating than blowing an otherwise brilliant ascent by pinging off an 'easy' move at the end that you were too lazy to check out. It happens.

"On extreme routes, a skilled belayer is an integral part of a successfully rehearsed and completed free ascent. This means more than knowing how much slack to pay out and shouting words of encouragement. It means performing the physical tasks of springing, serving as a counterweight to aid in pulling the leader up to a high bolt, and quickly pulling a leader off when he or she is ready to jump down to try a sequence again. It can also mean hours of tedium that are often essential for bagging extreme routes. My advice is to find a partner who is equally interested in working a route, and trade off the belaying duties between mutual attempts. There is nothing like needing a good belay to make someone put the effort into learning how to give one."

INJURIES

As the technical envelope is pushed further, debilitating injuries become more commonplace. Aside from the normal muscle tweaks and strains inherent in all sports, climbers particularly are prone to elbow and finger injuries, most of which involve some form of tendonitis. Having suffered these impairments on several occasions, I can assure you that ignoring the injury can result in pain so intense that straight-

ening the arm, or closing the fingers, is virtually impossible—
and climbing is out of the question.

Time and patience are the key ingredients to full recovery.
Returning prematurely to high-stress climbing is as foolish as
ignoring the injury in the first place. "The tissues of the mus-
culo-skeletal system are capable of remarkable feats of repair
and restoration," Dr. Mark Robinson (a climber and medical
authority) assures us, "but these processes are slow."
Furthermore, there is absolutely no proof that anything in
legitimate medicine can accelerate these processes, save the
use of anti-inflammatory drugs, which simply eliminate the
restrictions and allow the natural healing to proceed. But use
these drugs sparingly: recent studies indicate that ibupropfen
softens the connecting tissues, making you more susceptible
to injury. Again, all the fancy gadgets and expensive therapy
don't really accomplish a damn thing for tendon injuries.
Understand that if you have good insurance, you probably
will be referred to a sports medicine clinic. Such establish-
ments are not in business to refuse your money. I've (J.L.)
gone through the whole routine at a famous clinic, and after
several months was no better off than if I'd simply bought a
bottle of Aleve, and spent two months in the library reading
Spy Magazine. In extreme or very specific cases, an injection
of time-release cortisone can work wonders. But it can also do
more damage than good. Each injury is a little different, and
there is no generic verdict on the long-term effectiveness of
cortisone. My father, a surgeon, told me that whenever you
try to rush nature, you invariably run into problems. The
safest bet is to go the conservative route, and simply wait out
the injury.

Concerning treatment for chronic tendonitis, Dr. Robinson
(who has conducted several studies involving climbing
injuries) writes:

"Do the following to self-cure tendonitis:

• Decrease activity until the pain is gone, and all swelling
and tenderness disappear;

• Wait two weeks more;

• Start back with easy strength exercises—putty, gum,
rubber squeezers—for two-to-three weeks;

• Do low-angle, big-hold climbing for one month;

• Move to high-angle big-hold climbing for one month;

• Get back to full bore.

"Anti-inflammatory medicines (aspirin, Motrin and
Naprosyn) can be used to control symptoms and speed the
recovery process. They should not be used to suppress pain
to allow even more use, since this eventually will lead to more
problems and a longer recovery period.

"Various mystical and pseudo-scientific remedies, such as
dietary modifications, herbal cataplasms, spinal manipula-
tions, electrical machines with imposing control panels, horse
lineaments, and ethnic balms are at best unproven. Very few,
if any of them, bear any conceivable relation to what is known
to be the basis of the problem."

Injury Prevention

We know that the medical experts have told us that certain exercises virtually assure injuries, and that we should avoid these if we're in for the long haul. But aside from that, what can we do? Some support of critical tendons can be achieved by taping. Trouble spots include around the fingers on either side of the main (second) joint, around the wrist, and around the forearm, just shy of the elbow. But professional athletes are relying more and more on two things to avoid injuries: stretching and warming up. Aerobics and yoga might not make you stronger, but they may keep you from getting injured. And a very important practice is to do a little stretching and some easy climbing before jumping onto the main event. Warming up is part of any sport, and should be essential for climbers, whose movements so stress the elbows and fingers. This is particularly true for bouldering. Get limbered up and try and crack a light sweat, then max yourself. And if you tweak something, stop before you make it worse.

Kevin Powell photo

This warm-up ritual is vital for those returning from an injury, or nursing a chronic problem. For instance, I have always loved dynamic bouldering, but years of wrenching latches have left me with small bone chips in my right elbow. Specialists have said orthoscopic surgery might help things, but have advised me to just deal with the stiffness until the problem becomes unbearable. If I warm up, the pain usually subsides. If not, it's torturous.

Skin

Skin care is key to keep your fingers callused. The preferred method is determined by the type of climbing your doing and on what type of wall you're cranking. For instance, super-steep routes tend to work your second and third digits more than your tips; lower-angled face climbing will primarily work your tips. When your calluses build up too much, it is helpful to file them down (carefully!) with a pumice stone or drugstore file (the kind used specifically for removing heavy calluses). Let those callouses go and you risk ripping off huge chunks of skin/callous. Go easy on the file/pumice stone, however. Two strokes too many and you're into the wood.

Beth Wald photo

Nutrition

Beware the dangers of the strength-to-weight ratio. There are unspoken tragedies of eating disorders in climbing, as in any activity that relies so thoroughly on strength to weight. A five pound difference can make a world of difference, not to mention a 10-20 -pound difference; but remember that getting too thin and starving ones' self will make you weaker, and is a true health hazard to boot. Without proper nutrition, your blood sugar plummets, depleting your mental capacities and ability to strategize—to say nothing of losing power. And with binging and purging—which is more common than you might think in the sport climbing world—you lose so many necessary nutrients that it's impossible to function at a high level. No amount of vitamins will help to replace what you lose through binging/purging. Eating disorders can be fatal by themselves. When mixed with climbing, they are double trouble. Remember it is not only you at risk. Climbing is a partnership.

Vittles

Eating wisely and taking a balanced approach is usually the best solution to longevity. It takes more discipline to be balanced over the long run, than to be an occasional extremist. Extremism, especially in eating, always backfires in one way or another. Find balance and you will win on every front. We all have to be grateful for where we are and not judge ourselves harshly, even if Johnny is 10 pounds lighter and cranking harder. It doesn't matter in the big picture. We're all doing the same thing, and every move is a miracle. It's a matter of perception and appreciation.

Nutrition is so involved and specialized that a climber should approach the topic as a separate study. Much of the best information is published in body-building magazines (also a good source for training tips). A few trips to the library can help round out your program.

Many climbers eat whatever they can get their hands on,but, as mentioned, a growing number literally are starving themselves to achieve what they believe will be a greater strength-to-weight ratio. The fact is, everyone has a natural body weight. It's part of your genetic make-up. You can cheat it briefly by reducing calories and eliminating fats altogether; but it's a fact that below a certain point (in terms of body fat percentage), it's a game of diminishing returns. Also, trying to keep yourself that lean year-round is an inferior and downright stupid training philosophy. No athlete can peak for anything but brief periods of time. The key here is "brief." If you look at any other sport, you'll see that no athlete tries to maintain either top form or "fighting" weight the year-round. Not only is it impossible, it's counter-productive. Your performance should go in phases and cycles, and your weight should as well. That's not to say you should follow a good showing at Arco with a six-month binge of Dr. Pepper and Mars bars. The best athletes maintain good fitness and diet year-round. But they're experienced and smart enough to realize that both physically and mentally, you've got to give your body a break at least half the time.

The Mental Factor

Ten Ton Psyche

If you're out to challenge yourself, your best results will (almost always) come only when you truly feel like doing it. One of the best things about climbing is that it's altogether unofficial. You climb what you want, when you want. It's inevitable that as you get more involved in the sport, you will set certain goals for yourself. Eventually, you will head for the cliff with a particular route in mind. You'll say, I'm going to meet Shawn at the Sham Rock and we're going to climb Blarney. As a rule, the closer Blarney is to your technical limit, the more unpredictable your success. That's because there's no telling how you'll feel, physically or mentally, once you get to Sham Rock. You may have psyched yourself up for a week, worked out diligently, consumed tonics and herbs, chanted, got down on your knees and prayed to the Good Lord, yet all was for naught because on that particular day, you felt flat—just weren't into it—despite all the preparations. The best-laid plans and all that. Despite "common sense," a spontaneous decision is often the most productive. For example:

I had been trying to complete a new route at a local crag for some months, but always got stopped cold at the last crux. I had tried every conceivable approach, even camping at the base, but still it was no go. Finally, I gave up. Some months later, I was at the same crag. I had been to a bachelor party the previous night, and was working off two hours sleep and the ass end of a lot of hard liquor. Feeling smoked, I went with easy routes in the morning. After a couple hours, I inexplicably started feeling sharp and was anxious to turn up the heat. When we walked past the climb that had repeatedly routed me, I simply knew the time was perfect for another go. I couldn't walk by. I had to try it right then and there. I felt like I could do it, and that conviction grew into a "Ten Ton Psyche." I hadn't planned on trying the route until that very second. That day, I finally bagged it.

The point is, there is no way to predict when you'll feel like charging the lions. But when you do, realize it and make your move. You often see this phenomenon in track and field. Perhaps lately a runner has not been getting the marks he's expected. Maybe he's not even peaked for the race. Yet for unknown reasons, on a given night, everything comes together for him. He grabs the moment and a record falls. There was no predicting it, as there rarely is with the breaking of records. Most every track athlete performs best in practice.

When he tries to predict a world record, how often does he come through? Rarely, if ever. That's because it's impossible for even a world-class athlete to predict how he will feel at a given meet. But with climbing, there need not be a meet for it to count—everything counts. So if you're walking past a route that previously has humbled you, but you presently feel like you've simply got to try it, if you've got the Ten Ton Psyche, disregard your other plans. Jump on that route then and there. Get it while you're hot.

Ian Spencer-Green on "La Specialiste," 14a, Verdon Gorge, France.

Stewart M. Green photo

MENTAL MUSCLE

Take two climbers of the same ability and fitness. The one with the "right head" will prove the superior climber every time. She's the one who knows how to program her mind for performance. She may do this through imaging, visualization, self-hypnosis, relaxation techniques, and a host of other methods (some fatuous as smoky crystals), all of which long have been used by athletes to gain a mental edge. Particularly with climbing, where fear can paralyze your strength and resolve, a positive mental state is a basic ingredient to success, and it's mandatory for really hard climbing. Even a God-like mind cannot conquer physical limitations (no one climbs a wall with no holds, for instance), but an optimum mental state can greatly enhance genuine physical abilities.

The problem is, How do we weed through all the copper rhino horns, incense and mantras? How do we separate all the superfluity and rubbish from the few viable techniques that actually can help us? The surest way is to go with what has consistently worked best for most climbers.

From a practical standpoint, we need to know what the notions are and how to employ them to positively improve our climbing. Never mind the grad school lingo. We don't need a thesis, rather a guide, a mental recipe—tangible, straightforward and easily understood.

And that's what Eric Hörst has given us. Eric is a world-class climber who's published a series of excellent articles on the subject of how the mind influences performance. I've asked Eric to boil it all down and serve up the bare jewels. Says Eric:

"The biggest weapon we have in our quest for peak performance is our mind. It controls everything we do. At top levels, a properly programmed mind is tantamount to success; a poorly programed one, to failure.

"The muscles of our body need training to increase strength. The same is true for our 'mental muscle.' However, the benefits of mental training are less tangible than, say, lifting weights. It often requires more discipline to maintain a regular schedule of mental workouts.

"Our goals are the mastery of relaxation, centering and visualization. We accomplish this by practicing specific techniques and rituals, simply explained in the three tables that follow. But let's first look at relaxation, centering and visualization in fundamental terms, and get a firm grasp of the concepts.

Relaxation

"Here, our principal aim is the reduction of stress and dispensable muscular tension. Superfluous tension results in over-gripped holds, poor balance and a non-fluid, rigid style. Hard moves become harder because improper (non-specific) muscular tension unavoidably pits one muscle against the others.

"Optimal efficiency ia accomplished by relaxing all but the muscles necessary for the given motion. This accomplished, we greatly increase the cranking might of the 'task muscles.'

"This is an acquired skill. First, we learn "progressive relaxation," a procedure for relaxing the entire body in a mat-

---

THE PROGRESSIVE RELAXATION SEQUENCE

Perform the following procedure at least once a day. At first, it will take about 15 minutes—with practice, much less. Be sure to flex *only* the muscle(s) specified in each step—this is a valuable skill quickly learned. For rapid results, make a tape of these steps (one step per minute), and play it back as you perform the sequence.

1. Go to a quiet room and sit or lie in a comfortable position.
2. Close your eyes, take five deep breaths, and feel yourself 'let go.'
3. Tense the muscles in your lower leg (one leg at a time) for five seconds. Become aware of the feeling, then 'let go,' and relax the muscle completely. Recognize the difference between feeling tense and relaxed.
4. Perform the same sequence with the muscles in the upper leg. Tense for five seconds...then relax. Compare the difference.
5. Move to the arms. Start below the elbow, making a tight fist for five seconds, then relax.
6. Tense the muscles of the upper arm (one gun at a time)...and relax.
7. Move to the torso. As you get better, try to isolate and tense the chest, shoulder, back, and stomach muscles separately.
8. Finish by tensing the face and neck. Relax them completely, noting the feeling of relaxation in each part.
9. Now, concentrate on relaxing every muscle in your body. Scan from head to toe for any muscles that might still be tense. Maintain this state of total relaxation for at least three minutes.
10. Open your eyes, stretch, and feel refreshed; or begin visualization and imagery work; or go to sleep!

ter of minutes (See table). Once that is mastered, we quickly can learn "differential relaxation," where we relax all but task-required muscles. With practice, we can accomplish this in the middle of a 5.14 crux. The concept is simple; doing so is not. Practice in the gym. For instance, when doing pull-ups, try relaxing everything but the pulling back and arm muscles, and so on.

"On the rock, experiment with different levels of muscular tension while both moving and resting. Strive to find the minimum level of contraction necessary to stay on the stone. Practice often. You'll soon climb with added grace and less effort. In time, the practice will become automatic.

Centering

Centering is a simple, yet effective means of gaining and maintaining optimum control of our mind and body as we start a difficult route. When we're centered, we feel strong, confident, relaxed, balanced and keenly aware of our center of gravity.

"Centering requires us to focus our thoughts inward, mentally checking and adjusting our breathing and level of muscular tension. Do this regularly, and you'll learn to counteract any involuntary changes that may have occurred due to the pressure of the situation (like hyperventilation, over- gripping, sewing-machine leg, etc.).

THE INSTANT CENTERING SEQUENCE (ICS)

The ICS should be performed in an upright position—either sitting or standing. You can perform the sequence almost anytime or anywhere, as long as your eyes are open and you're alert. At first, take a few minutes and slowly go through the steps. With practice, you'll eventually be able to do it in a second or two.

1. Uninterrupted Breathing: Continue your current breathing cycle, concentrating on smooth, deep, and even breaths.
2. Positive Face: Flash a smile, no matter your mental state. Research shows that a positive face 'resets' the nervous system so that it's less reactive to negative stress. You'll feel the difference immediately.
3. Balanced Posture: Lift your head up, shoulders broad and loose, back comfortably straight, and abdomen free of tension. A balanced posture makes you feel light, with a sense of no effort in action. A tense and collapsed posture restricts breathing, reduces blood flow, slows reactions, and magnifies negative feelings.
4. Wave of Relaxation: Perform a 'tension check.' Scan all your muscles in a quick sweep to locate unnecessary tension. Let go of those tensions, making your body calm while your mind remains alert.
5. Mental Control: Be focused, positive, and uninhibited about the task at hand. Acknowledge reality, and go with the flow!

"The most effective method of centering is the "Instant Calming (or Centering) Sequence" (ICS). This simple, five-step procedure (see table) provides us with exceptional inner control, even in the face of grim runouts. The ICS is simple to learn and use, especially if you've mastered the aforementioned relaxation techniques. Initially, it will take some minutes to perform; with practice you can get centered in a matter of seconds, or even with a single breath.

"Use the ICS any time you feel rushed, stressed, or scared. Practice at home, or at work—the more you practice, the better and more effectively you can apply the skill to your climbing. Center yourself before every climb, and re-center at every shake-out or rest. This momentary clearing and readjustment will renew your control of mind and body, and enhance your performance on the remainder of the route.

Visualization

Proper visualization provides a mental blueprint for our bodies to execute. By creating and repeating this "mental movie," mentally watching ourselves flawlessly climb a given section, we program it into our mind as reality, and now have a tangible "experience," or guide, showing the way. Correctly visualizing ourselves climbing the crux is truly an invaluable aid, absolutely essential for extreme routes; accordingly, visualization is the most important exercise for attaining peak performance.

"You probably already are performing mental rehearsals of a route you are working on. Proper visualization, however,

VISUALIZATION STRATEGIES

1. Practice visualizing and imagining with all your senses. Work on developing your ability to create vivid mental pictures of people, places, and events. The more you practice, the better you will get.

2. Imagine your senses in explicit detail. Remember, the more vivid the image, the more powerful the effect.

3. Use photographs, beta sheets, or videotape to improve the accuracy of the mental movies of yourself climbing.

4. Mentally practice many times the sequence or climb that gives you the most problems. Remember that the physical practice of a sequence, when combined with mental practice, will yield much greater results than if you just physically worked it.

5. Create lots of strong positive images, while eliminating images of failure.

6. Create mental movies of yourself dealing with various situations or problems that might arise on a climb.

7. Work hard every day to change and reconstruct your negative and self-defeating images to positive and constructive ones.

8. Most importantly, establish a regular visualization practice schedule, just as you have a regular gym workout schedule.

goes far beyond the easy task of reviewing crux sequences. Try to create detailed "movies" of touch, sound, and color, along with the kinesthetic "feel" of actually doing moves. Even imagine the shake-outs and rests, where you will perform the relaxation and centering techniques discussed earlier.

"To learn visualization, imagine yourself climbing from an observer's point of view. Watch yourself performing the moves perfectly—smooth and effortlessly—from bottom to top. Imagine clearly even the slightest details, and incorporate positive images of "flow" and being "right-on." Nix any negative and self-defeating images, because these glitches can easily become reality.

"With practice, you'll soon be able to perform internal visualization, where you envision every detail as you would see it through your own eyes. This creates a very detailed mental movie by dint of the tactile feel of grabbing holds and pulling through successive moves. The ultimate goal is total mind/body integration, best accomplished through creating these mental movies. (More on this in the table of visualization strategies.) Visualization particularly is valuable when used to pre-program for an on-sight ascent. Be creative here. Visualize not only doing the moves, but placing the gear, chalking up, resting, and of course, topping out.

Conclusion

"All of these mental techniques give a climber a decided edge over someone who simply walks up to a route and climbs. As mentioned, said techniques are acquired skills, and initially require the same effort and discipline as working out in the gym. Once mastered, however, they require little time and effort to maintain. Practice them regularly and you're guaranteed major improvements in your climbing skill; without them, you'll never realize your full potential. Remember that the best athletes are not those with something added, but rather those with very little of their potential taken away."

For best results, visualization should be practiced when you are relaxed and in a quiet place. Many short sessions each week are better than just one or two long sessions.

Climbers interested in further study should refer to the two texts used by Hörst to fabricate his tables: *Mental Toughness Training For Sports,* by James E. Loehr, 1986, The Stephen Greene Press, Lexington, MA.; and *Health & Fitness Excellence,* by Robert Cooper, 1989, Houghton Mifflin Co., Boston, MA. Plus Hörst's two books in the How To Rock Climb Series: *How to Climb 5.12,* and *Flash Training.*

Our main man Eric Hörst has plotted a clear and direct course for us to maximize our "mental muscle." Note that the course involves very specific techniques. We do not stare at a zircon pyramid, or repeat a mouthful of hogwash. There is no wheatgrass or ethnic balm involved, no chanting to the moon. Just the basic, time-proven stuff here. Stick with Hörst's techniques, and see tangible improvements in your climbing. Guaranteed.

The only thing I might add is a little more slippery and far less defined. Should you have any spiritual convictions, orthodox or simply your own, dial them up them before starting up a route. All wise hearts, all creeds, agree about one thing—that life involves far more than climbing rocks. Be glad you're alive, healthy and with friends. Put the route in perspective. Granted, an extreme climb requires the tenacity of a polecat from hell; but it's still just a rock climb. If you hang your identity on having to succeed, you only create undo pressures, and apprehensions of failing. If you're not afraid to fail, you probably won't. And if you can't nail the route that day, that hardly spells a washout. Who's stopping you from returning to try again another day? Never mind that Pepe de la Gaffo flashed the thing. To heck with Pepe and the burro he rode in on. Get relaxed, centered, visualize your success, acknowledge that climbing is a fabulous aspect of a multifarious life—but no more—then go after that route with a vengeance!

Evolution of a Champion

The world's greatest climbers started just like you and I did—by taking a beginner's class, holding a cousin's rope, getting pulled up a host of climbs by a friend. Sometime, probably early on, the champion makes the first important realization—that he or she loves climbing. He starts climbing more, masters basic ropework, and slowly hones technique. He might be a natural, but probably not. The most important ingredient is desire. If the desire endures and he gets totally hooked, then it's full immersion: hitch-hiking to the boulders if there's no ride; climbing with anyone, anywhere; and boning up on all the literature down to analyzing guidebooks while on the toilet.

Goals are soon set—like breaking into 5.8. That accomplished, many routes are possible. The climber starts dreaming about scaling this one or that, and more tangible goals are drawn into focus. As the climber starts checking off the routes and moving through the grades, his progress is pretty uniform and increases relative to how much he climbs. The first major hurdle comes at 5.10. For years, this was the magic number, signifying entrance into a sort of mythical zone of difficulty. Though climbing 5.10 is commonplace nowadays, it doesn't seem so when a climber first gets there. These climbs are hard, and require a stout effort regardless of the climber's ability. The next phase is 5.11. Even today, when huge numbers are passé, the climber who can go to any area, climb any kind of rock at a 5.11 standard—from off-size cracks to slab routes—is a rare bird. The last hurdle is at 5.13, which is the threshold into world-class turf. Here, even the phenomenal natural athlete will really have to buckle down, because everyone regularly climbing 5.13 is a natural athlete. Moving past 5.13 requires raw toil and intense mileage on the rock, and, normally, a withering training schedule on artificial walls as well; and even these cannot guarantee a champion. The key is the rarest ingredient of them all—the champion's mentality. Without it, the strongest, the bravest, the most talented natural climber ever born will never make a lasting mark. This mindset can be drawn out but never realized unless a climber has a little of it latently. One eventually will find out if he has that latent mindset, provided his desire is keen enough. It rarely is, however, because steadfast dedication is very hard to sustain.

The distractions and elemental needs of living in today's world defeat most potential champions. Like most of us who set out to vanquish the climbing world, the aspiring champ will find it difficult enough just to keep his van running. It's a mat-

(opposite)

Diane French at Shelf Road, Colorado.

Beth Wald photo

ter of money—or the lack of it—that keeps the bulk of us "weekend warriors" out of the running. The basic cost of living is so high that the Bohemian life once enjoyed by "crag rats" now is economically impossible. In the early '70s, a climber could go to Yosemite with a couple hundred dollars, climb the whole summer and drink beer every night. If you had $500, you could live like a Pharaoh, and maybe go on an expedition or two. But those days are gone forever, and anyone trying to live like that is pushed so far to the fringe of things that there is little distinguishing him from a bag person, kicking around the crags with a skimpy rack and a few cans of chickpeas in his tattered pack. And that is no way to live. Moreover, it's virtually impossible to maintain a controlled and disciplined lifestyle—so essential for the world-class athlete—without a place to hang your hat, to cook, shower, and relax. And even if you have the discipline and resources, even if you have the desire and God-given ability, so very few are willing to sacrifice virtually everything for climbing.

Those men and women climbing at the very highest grade are, and have been, doing little else but climbing rocks and swinging in the gym for some years. They are fanatics who would never have gotten where they are if their climbing had not grown into a sort of all-consuming vice. Balzac said it costs as much to support a vice as it does to support a family. Those grappling toward the top will discover this; they must climb, climb, climb, at the exclusion of most everything else. There's little time for a job, a wife or husband, or even a fraction of what we know as the "good life." So you see, the odds are heavily stacked against anyone ever becoming a champion. Recurring injuries, a bad fall, a broken heart, simple burn out and feelings that life is passing you by—these things are lurking in the shadows, and virtually every champion must wage a pitched battle against any and all of them.

Yet despite all the hurdles and sacrifices, despite the million-to-one odds of it ever happening, a few champions always emerge. Through pure willpower, they kick down the barriers and give the rest of us things to marvel at. But the bona fide champion is more than just a fabulous technical climber. His best climbs are monuments to the human spirit, pivotal ascents that reorient and redefine the game. Because of this, he's a symbolic ambassador for everyone who owns a rope and a pair of boots. And he'll feel the heat of all the eyes upon him. The fool will say he could climb like that if he only had the time. The jealous, cowed by such passion, or suspicious of another's praise, will scoff and look for fault and shortcomings. He'll find them, of course, but he's missed the point— that it takes a miracle to become a champion. But how easy it is to criticize. A little wit, mixed with ill-nature, confidence and malice, will do it. But to everyone who has ever perused a guidebook or a ghastly cliff and dreamed a dream, it's the champion's face that smiles back at them, assuring us that he was the one who actualized the dream. We don't worship him, because he's flesh-and-bone like all of us. For pure effort and remarkable accomplishment he deserves our praise; but he never demands it, for all the trials, failures, and pain have shown him that even his success is modest and fleeting. Knowing that his victory is ours as well, the champion is gracious. He does not rub our faces in his prowess—such a knave is not a champion, but simply a great climber. The genuine champion is far less vain than the climber who doesn't give a damn about who the champion is or what he or she has done.

The champion quickly will learn that it is much easier to become one than to remain one. It's never crowded at the top, but the queue is long and others are banging at the door. The game is for the young, and the champion can shine brightly only for so long. Realizing this, the champion attacks the crags with a mission, and makes his mark while he's hot. A little introspection will give him a sense of the proportion of things, so that when life finally catches up with him, he can climb on board. To doggedly try and hold out is not to live out a dream, but to foster a nightmare. The champion must realize when the time has come to move on. Not to is as tragic as if he had never climbed a single pitch. There are more things in life than climbing rocks, and he who thinks otherwise is bound to end up a loser, a bitter has-been hunkered down inside a wine bottle, for whom both climbing and life has passed by. After a time, he's unsuited for anything worthwhile. He simply didn't know when to get out and, like a fly in amber, he's stuck in no-man's land. The champion, then, is the one who knows when he's done all he can, or all he should, and who gracefully passes the garland and exits the way he came in—inspired, staunch, and true to the target. These things will hold him in good stead for the rest of his life. His victories have given him perspective. He leaves the sport in better shape than he found it, and we're all enriched by his contribution.

We'll still see him at the crags now and again. He'll climb as hard as he wants to, and we will all recognize him as the guy who's having the most fun. No doubt, the authentic champion is the rarest thing in all the climbing world.